Beyond Generative Grammar:

A COURSE IN PERFORMATIVE LINGUISTICS

Beyond Generative Grammar:

A COURSE IN PERFORMATIVE LINGUISTICS

M. K. C. UWAJEH
University of Benin
NIGERIA.

Spectrum Books Limited
Ibadan
Abuja • Benin City • Lagos • Owerri

Spectrum titles can be purchased on line at
www.spectrumbooksonline.com

Published by
Spectrum Books Limited
Spectrum House
Ring Road
PMB 5612
Ibadan, Nigeria

in association with
Safari Books (Export) Limited
1st Floor
17 Bond Street
St. Helier
Jersey JE2 3NP
Channel Islands
United Kingdom

Europe and USA Distributor
African Books Collective Ltd.
The Jam Factory
27 Park End Street
Oxford OX1, 1HU, UK

© M.K.C. Uwajeh

First published, 2002

All rights reserved. This book is copyright and so no part of it may be reproduced, stored in a retrieval system, or transmitted, in any form or by any means, electronic, mechanical, electrostatic, magnetic tape, photocopying, recording or otherwise, without the prior written permission of the copyright owner.

ISBN: 978-029-376-0

Printed by Polygraphics Venture Limited Ibadan

...In the end my case is not that Chomsky's theory is false, but that it is incomprehensible.

MATTHEWS, P. H. (1979:21):
Generative Grammar and Linguistic Competence

Contents

	Pages
Epigraph	v
Table of Figures	xiii

INTRODUCTION: **SAUSSURE'S LEGACY UPDATE**   1

CHAPTER ONE: **LANGUAGE AND LINGUISTICS**

Generative Grammar's theory of Language..................... 8
Characterising Language in Performative Linguistics........... 11

CHAPTER TWO: **GRAMMAR AND LINGUISTICS**

In Generative Grammar, Grammar = Linguistics............... 15
Language is essentially a communication tool 16

The distinctive character of linguistic communication 19
Language communication skills. 23
Intralinguistic communication skills 24
Linguistic construction and comprehension. 24
The distinctive character of representational relationships 27
Active Language Competence and
    Passive Language Competence 31
Extralinguistic communication skills 33
Linguistic competence and Linguistics 36

CHAPTER THREE: SEMANTICS AND GRAMMAR

Grammar = Structural Semantics + Structural Symbolics 39
Contextual Semantics is NOT part of Grammar 42
The domain of Semantics. 44
Conceptual Semantics. 45
What is a 'concept'? 45
Conceptual indeterminacy 47
Contrastive Conceptual Semantics. 50
Conceptual inconstancy. 50
Propositional Semantics 54

What is a 'proposition'?.. 56

Contrastive Propositional Semantics............................. 56

Propositions and world picture 58

The SAPIR-WHORF Hypothesis revisited....................... 60

Importance of respecting SL community's world picture 68

CHAPTER FOUR: SYNTAX AND GRAMMAR

In Generative Grammar, Syntax = Grammar 81

The domain of Syntax 85

Symbolics and Grammar 85

Speech and Symbolics 89

Towards dethroning the Primacy of Speech Principle 89

Speech and writing 91

The character of symbolisation 97

Elements of Graphetics 101

Nuclear Graphics 102

Equality of all Language forms 104

Syntax and Structural Symbolics 106

CHAPTER FIVE: THE LEXICON AND GRAMMAR

The Traditional Grammar foundation of
    Generative Grammar... 108
Lexical categorisation in modern Linguistics 110
The morphological means definition type 111
The syntactic means definition type 112
The composite features presentation approach 114
The bi-componential nature of lexical items 115

CHAPTER SIX: GRAMMAR AND PRAGMATICS

CHOMSKY's revolution in Linguistics 118
A psychologically real Grammar must be a
    Performance Grammar 119
Context-free Grammars cannot be psychologically real 122
A Performance Grammar is also necessarily a Competence
    Grammar... 123
Language text and Language context 127
The importance of context in Grammar 129
Beyond Generative Grammar 137

CONCLUSION:	**CHAOS THEORY IN LINGUISTICS**	138

WORKS CITED 147

INDEX 155

Table of Figures

		Pages
1.	Grammar, the Study of Language Structure — According to Generative Grammar..............................	9
2.	Language Structure, the Object Studied by Grammar — According to Generative Grammar.........................	10
3.	The Sign, the Fundamental Unit of Language	12
4.	Language, an Essentially Bicomponential (i.e., a Semantic- Symbolic) Phenomenon	14
5.	Linguistics = Semantics + Symbolics	14
6.	The Three Rs of Language Construction	26
7.	The Three Rs of Language Comprehension	27
8.	The Psychological or Immediate Context of Language Communication..	36
9.	Linguistics = Grammar + Pragmatics	38
10.	Grammar = Textual Semantics + Textual Symbolics...	42
11.	Pragmatics = Contextual Semantics + Contextual Symbolics..	42

12.	Linguistics = Textual Semantics and Contextual Semantics + Textual Symbolics and Contextual Symbolics	43
13a	The Sub-Disciplines of Semantics, I	55
13b	The Sub-Disciplines of Semantics, II.	55
14.	The Constituency of Symbolics...........................	100
15.	The Constituency of Structural Symbolics	107

INTRODUCTION: SAUSSURE'S LEGACY UPDATE

At the beginning of the twentieth century, Ferdinand de SAUSSURE's posthumously (1916) published book, *A Course in General Linguistics, (Cours de Linguistique Générale* in its original French title), changed radically thenceforth the conduct of Linguistics, and transformed irrevocably the discipline into a self-contained respectable science in its own right. The content of SAUSSURE's book was largely the material of his linguistic work in the last quarter of the nineteenth century – work which was in significant respects set in a scientific paradigm diametrically opposed to that of the most influential Linguists of his time, the Neogrammarian School of Linguists, who were obsessed with *linguistic evolution* in their exclusive preoccupation with Diachronics or *Historical Linguistics*, the hallmark of nineteenth-century Linguistics.

Key elements of SAUSSURE's intervention were as follows: first, on the elective **phenomenon** for the preoccupation of Linguistics, **Language** itself, NOT the **act** of using Language in speaking, is **the** object of its study, he said. Second, concerning **the intrinsic nature of Language** as the subject matter for elucidation in Linguistics, Language is **both** meaningful form **and** the meaning itself (i.e., the thought itself) expressed with that meaningful form — NOT just the meaningful form only. Third, about **the focus of investigation** in Linguistics science, the study is essentially **synchronic** (i.e., preoccupied with the **nature** of Language as a constant), NOT diachronic (i.e., NOT preoccupied with innumerable changes observed in languages over time) — the latter concern being incidental to and dependent upon the former. Fourth, as regards **the goal** of Linguistics as a science, the nature of the Language phenomenon **in itself and for itself**, NOT some other objective(s), is the only end of the study of Language in Linguistics as a science discipline.

Now at the beginning of the twenty-first century, this book, *A Course in Performative Linguistics*, is intended to update SAUSSURE's *A Course in General Linguistics* of the twentieth century and stipulate the recommended shape of Linguistics from the twenty-first century — by highlighting several key aspects of the nature of Language as a **social** phenomenon. The content of this book is largely the material of my linguistic work in the last quarter of the twentieth century — work which was in significant respects set in a scientific paradigm diametrically opposed to that of the most influential Linguists of our time, the Generative Grammar School of Linguists, who have to date been overly fascinated with what they call **syntax,** in their exclusive preoccupation with Grammar or **Structural Linguistics,** the hallmark of twentieth- century Linguistics. In the **syntacticist** characterisation of Language of (both Structuralism and) Generativism, the nature of Language is supposedly **fully** specified in its structure — such that linguistic description there is essentially communication context-**free;** and a particular illocution category, like 'exclamative' or 'interrogative' for instance, is attributed to a given sentence **because of** its structure, independently therefore of the sentence's communication context. In **Performativism**, my **pragmaticist** perspective for the characterisation of Language being advertised in these pages, the structure of Language is the textual part of the nature of Language — the other part being the contextual (or use) part; such that linguistic description there is necessarily context-**sensitive**, and a particular illocution category, like 'exclamative' or 'interrogative' for instance, attributed to a sentence construct is deducible from the contextual facts of the given language communication act, whereby the sentence structure itself is only **one and non-obligatory** way of manifesting the communicator's communicated illocutive intent in the language communication act. The key elements of this my proposed pragmaticist framework called *Performative Linguistics* may be stated generally as follows.

First, 'Performative' in 'Performative Linguistics' comes from 'performance': thus, Performative Linguistics is a **performance** Linguistics — that is, a Linguistics of **Language-as-it-is-used** type, like Text Linguistics. It is an approach to Linguistics which I started to work out in the late 1970s at the Université de Montréal, to help counter the perceived inherent inadequacies of Generativism's syntacticist characterisation of Language. The bedrock postulate of Performativism is that the Language phenomenon is a kind of **performance** (i.e., here, a kind of **something performed**, NOT the act of performing itself, as 'performance' is often nowadays understood) – an 'intelligent performance' to be exact, in this special sense that Language is something performed by its users with due regard for the communication exigencies of real life; such that Language texture or structure is in effect conditioned by and a reflection of those communicative constraints; therefore, that any realist characterisation of Language must also take into account those same communicative exigencies which make texts **bona fide** communicative constructs of Language users. Since language structure is **a performance** (i.e., a something 'performed'), and non-structural essentials of Language are indispensable for realising that construction, the cardinal tenet inherent in the notion of **performative** in Performative Linguistics is that **the nature of Language involves more than the structure of Language**.

Second, Language systems of communication are, according to Performative Linguistics, distinguishable from other semiotic systems by the fact that they are characteristically **representational**, while the latter are **indicational**. For a representational means of communication, information is **specified** with the means **by convention** – i.e., in such way that the information which the means expresses is **knowable in advance**, as it were by agreement between the users of the means, prior to the actual use of that means in real life situations. For an indicational means of communication, information is **implied** with the means **in context** – i.e., in an **ad hoc** way, such that the information which the means expresses is deduced by observers of that means from the peculiar circumstances of that particular communication. According to Performative Linguistics, therefore, indication is the **general** means of communication open to **all** communicating individuals, while representation is the **specialised** means of communication restricted to Language-using individuals.

Third, in Performative Linguistics Language content comprises **both** a thought (or meaning) component **and** a symbolisation (or form) component – with NOTHING ELSE in between, or apart from, these two constituents as regards the Language phenomenon. Syntax is **NOT** a third constituent of Language, supposedly separate somehow from Language meaning and Language form, as has been posited in Generative Grammar for more than forty years now, but is in fact **an aspect of Language form** – i.e. the aspect of Language concerning the organization (or external structuring) of words in linguistic communication. The relationship between Language form and Language meaning is one of **representation**, according to Performative Linguistics – the form being the **representer** and the meaning, the **represented**. As the twentieth century drew to a close in the 1990s, it was gratifying for me to note that Generativism, in its so-called 'Minimalist Program' (MP) phase of Grammar, had begun to envisage a basically two-part (meaning-form) constituency **only** for Language make-up, wherein syntax ceases to have the overwhelming importance earlier attributed to it as a supposed third major constituent of Language – in line with the position of Performative Linguistics I have been stating categorically at the University of Benin since 1980.

Fourth, symbolisation (i.e., the form part of Language content) is **neither** necessarily **nor** primarily speech in Performative Linguistics. Put slightly differently, the so-called Primacy of Speech Principle in modern Linguistics (whereby **spoken** language is supposedly **the** real object for Linguistics) is **wrong**, according to the shape of Linguistics being recommended here as a matter of course from the twenty-first century: for Language is NOT **by its nature** necessarily spoken – rather than gestural or written, say. In this viewpoint, **all symbolisation systems are equal** as meaning-expressing means; none is ''more equal'' than another inherently; rather, each symbolisation system type is functionally superior or inferior to another depending on which specific communication need of the language communicator is being targeted. For example, written Language was ostensibly superior in history to spoken Language for keeping records; but written Language is still manifestly inferior in speed of communication to spoken Language, generally speaking. Similarly, gestural Language appears to have the advantage over spoken Language of being usable by both deaf-mutes and other persons non-handicapped in that specific respect; but the fact that speech does **not** obligatorily require visual contact between communicator and communicatee clearly renders speech functionally superior to gestural Language in the specific respect just highlighted.

Now to close this panoramic but short presentation. At the beginning of the twentieth century, Ferdinand de SAUSSURE demonstrated with erudite clarity how Linguistics derives its status as a **science** from its sole preoccupation with **the nature of Language**; at this beginning of the twenty-first century, I wish to establish how Linguistics derives its status as **a social science** from its preoccupation with **both** the structural **and** non-structural constituents of the nature of Language. In this task, I shall confront specifically several (but by no means all of the) weaknesses of Generative Grammar's syntacticist characterisation of Language, and recommend therefrom the Performative Linguistics perspective for Linguistic Theory. In short, while SAUSSURE was concerned with laying down, contrary to the tenets of the Neogrammarian School of Linguistics, the general condition for studying the Language phenomenon which is required of a truly scientific Linguistics (i.e., the condition that the study preoccupies itself solely with **the nature** of Language), my own goal here in this book is to recommend, contrary to the tenets of the Generative Grammar School of Linguistics, the specific condition for studying that same Language phenomenon which is inevitable for a truly productive Linguistics **social science** (viz, the condition that the study preoccupies itself with **both** the structure and **use** of Language as a **social** tool). Therefore, my *Course in Performative Linguistics* should be best appreciated as the logical successor to SAUSSURE's *Course in General Linguistics*.

CHAPTER **1**

LANGUAGE AND LINGUISTICS

Generative Grammar's theory of Language

The goal of Linguistics science is the theory of Language, also called "Linguistic Theory" – that is, the elucidation of the nature of Language; in other words, characterising Language, or determining what Language really is. My general driving motivation for writing this book is to demonstrate conclusively that the theory of Language proffered by Generative Grammar is irremediably flawed; and my set objective throughout the book is accordingly to suggest what the correct alternative theory should look like.

Although Generative Grammarians are rather wary about defining 'Language' in terms other than those of 'sets of sentences', it is incontrovertibly evident from virtually all serious mainstream treatises of this School of Linguists since CHOMSKY's (1965) *Aspects of the Theory of Syntax* that if Grammar as the study of Language structure is envisaged within the Generative scientific paradigm to be a **tripartite**[1] entity

---

1. Even the first version of the Grammar (then called simply "Transformational

comprising a syntactic component, a semantic component, and a phonological component, then Language, which Grammar models, must also be a **tripartite object** comprising a syntactic constituent, a semantic constituent, and a phonological constituent – as follows:

GRAMMAR

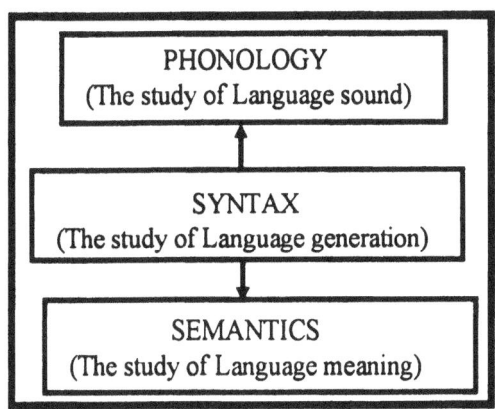

Fig. 1: Grammar, the Study of Language Structure — According to Generative Grammar

---

Grammar"), in CHOMSKY's (1957) *Syntactic Structures*, which eloquently ignored semantic considerations in the characterisation of Language structure, still managed to posit a *tripartite* framework. One notable exception to this tripartite scheme appears with the latest Minimalist Programme (MP) phase of Generative Grammar (see CHOMSKY, 1995), where Grammar is for the first time conceived in terms of a bipartite framework - as follows:

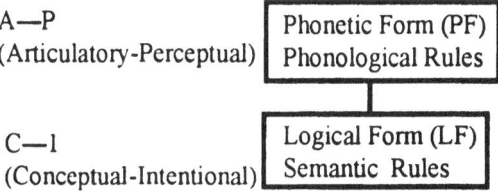

LANGUAGE

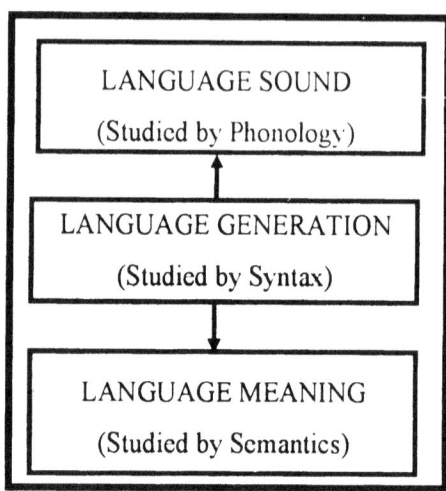

Fig. 2: Language Structure, the Object Studied by Grammar – According to Generative Grammar.

However, for as long as Generative Grammar has not categorically renounced its tenet of an interpretive semantics (whereby sentences are essentially syntactic constructs, that may then be interpreted semantically or phonologically), and for as long as the paradigm has not made a definite statement as to where the perennial "generative" syntactic component is now re-located (and if it has disappeared entirely, what replaces it now), this incredible conversion of Generative Grammar to a bicomponential model of Language must remain thoroughly suspect for quite some time – i.e., until we know where "syntax" has gone.

Furthermore, even in the (now moribund) Generative Semantics version of Generative Grammar where there is no separate syntactic component as such – the entire set of rules of the Grammar being generative – there is still a **third** (also "syntactic"?) so-called "Transformational Component" mediating between the semantic base and the phonological surface of Grammar.

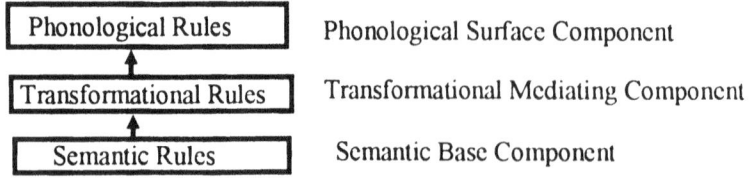

This standard characterisation of Language by Generative Grammar cannot be a true theory of Language because it introduces a third, **fictitious** component (i.e., the generative or syntactic component) into Language's make-up, which renders the Language phenomenon essentially **incomprehensible** to commonsense. Since this third so-called generative or syntactic component of Language concerns the processes (or "rules" in Generative Grammar terminology), and these processes actually apply **either** to sounds **or** to meanings in the paradigm, it is obvious that the so-called third component is actually **both** part of the meaning component **and** part of the sound component – i.e., (i) the units of sound and the processes of relating sound units to one another should constitute one main component of Language, while (ii) the units of meaning **and** the processes of relating meaning units to one another should constitute the other major component of Language. Language should thus have TWO, **and only two**, immediate constituents in its make-up – which is the Linguistic Theory of Performative Linguistics I advance and justify in this book.

Characterising Language in Performative Linguistics

So, what is 'Language' according to Performative Linguistics? Language may be said to be 'any system-structure of signs for the communication of experiences'. By ''experiences'' here I refer to any preoccupations communicated (with Language), **not** to the experiencing activities themselves of the mind. Also, in this definition, a ''sign'' is strictly understood not to consist of sound form only, but to comprise **both** an idea, technically known as a *concept* (which is a fundamental unit of **thought**, or of "meaning" according to traditional usage) and a symbol, or what I may specially designate here by the technical term *seme* (which is the corresponding fundamental unit of **symbolisation**, or of "form" in traditional parlance), representing the concept.[2]

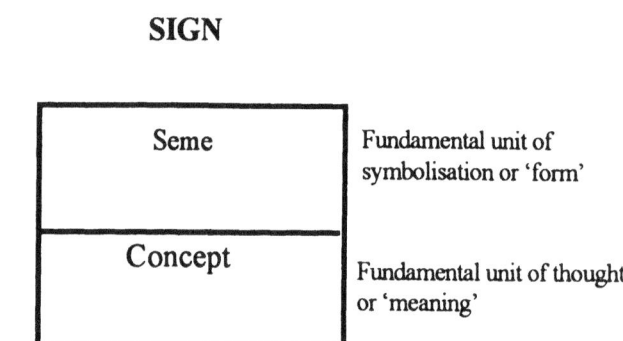

Fig. 3: The Sign, the Fundamental Unit of Language

---

2. The definition of Language here in this chapter is roughly in line with the teaching of the great Swiss Linguist Ferdinand de SAUSSURE in his posthumously published *Cours de Linguistique Générale* (1916); Payot, Paris. SAUSSURE emphasised the intrinsic **semantic-symbolic** (i.e., meaning-form) bicomponential nature of Language highlighted in my definition of Language above by comparing Language to a sheet of paper with its two and only two sides: one of the 'sides' of Language is thus 'meaning', while the other is 'form'; and just as you cannot tear off a piece of the paper without taking something of the two sides, so each essential unit of Language necessarily has a meaning (or thought) part and a form (or symbolisation) part to it.

Language may also be defined, more succinctly, like this: 'any semantic-symbolic intercommunication representational system-structure'. As a 'system', Language is a representational semantic-symbolic (i.e., thought-and-symbolisation or meaning-and-form) **potentiality** – that is, any composite of units of thought as well as the ways of relating them to one another **and** any composite of units of symbolisation (not necessarily phonic) as well as the ways of relating them to one another, representing the thought, that are 'stored' in the minds of individuals (who may be non-human), waiting to be used in appropriate situations of real life. As a structure, Language is that same representational semantic-symbolic system now made an actuality – that is , the semantic **and** symbolic constituents and relations specified above now 'performed' by the individuals in whose minds they are stored as knowledge actually communicating thereby with one another in real life. In short, Language is a system-structure of thought (traditionally called "meaning") **and** its corresponding system-structure of symbolisation (traditionally called "form", which is **not necessarily** sound) representing the thought, for the communication of life's preoccupations that we may technically refer to as 'experiences'.

From the above presentation, we can see that Language has two, and only two, immediate constituents – (i) a semantic or thought (i.e., 'meaning') component, and (ii) a symbolic or symbolisation (i.e., 'form') component representing the thought – for communication.

LANGUAGE

SYMBOLISATION or 'form'
THOUGHT or 'meaning'

Fig. 4: Language, an Essentially Bicomponential (i.e. a Semantic-Symbolic) Phenomenon.

This is a fact of singular importance to remember in Linguistics; for it implies that any scientific study of Language must concern only these two constituents essentially. It follows that Linguistics may be neatly divided into (i) the study of thought (or 'meaning'), **Semantics,** and (ii) the study of symbolisation (or 'form'), **Symbolics**:

LINGUISTICS

SYMBOLICS, the scientific study of Symbolisation /'form'
SEMANTICS, the scientific study of Thought/'meaning'

Fig. 5: Linguistics = Semantics + Symbolics

CHAPTER **2**

GRAMMAR AND LINGUISTICS

In Generative Grammar, Grammar = Linguistics

Because the **structure** of Language is the essential thing about Language in Generative Grammar's 'syntacticist' study of Language,[1] it is standard practice for Generative Grammarians to characterise Language as if linguistic **structure** competence were the same thing as linguistic competence **as a whole**, and as if Linguistic Theory, the goal of Linguistics, were the same thing as Grammatical Theory (also called 'Grammar' in the paradigm), the goal of Grammar.[2] The result of the above lamentable methodological lapse is that in Generative Grammar, it is commonplace to find statements which make Grammar, that part of Linguistics concerned with describing

---

1. Cf. CHOMSKY, N. (1975:55-58).

2. cf. CHOMSKY, N. (1965: 24)

   A grammar can be regarded as a theory of a language; it is **descriptively adequate** to the extent that it correctly describes the intrinsic competence of the idealized native speaker.

15

Language structure competence, the whole of the discipline concerned with describing Language competence in its totality.[3]

A whole is of course NOT equal to one of its parts; and so, Generative Grammar's syntacticist Linguistic Theory fails in general because **there is much more to Linguistics than the study of Language structure.** In this chapter, I specify in some detail **what else** Linguistics does study besides Language structure, and the importance of that study for the characterisation of Language or linguistic competence.

Language is essentially a communication tool

One of the essential non-structural features of Language is the fact that it is **a communication tool**. To know any language – that is, to have any given language competence – is to have acquired certain **communication skills**, or to have acquired a type of communication competence, because the primary and inalienable function of any language is that of communication. Thus, there are **two**[4] parties in any instance of Language use –

---

3   cf. CHOMSKY, N. (1965: 5):

  A grammar of a language purports to be a description of the ideal speaker-hearer's intrinsic competence.

4   The same individual may assume the role of the two parties (of communicator and communicatee) as in soliloquy. Also, the communicator party and/or communicatee party may be made up of more than one individual (respectively) - for example, you have many persons constituting the communicator party when many spectators at a football match ask their favourite team to score more goals; and there are many persons in the communicatee party when it consists of a crowd of angry persons being addressed by their union leader.

(i) an information sender-party, called the 'communicator', and (ii) an information receiver-party, called the 'communicatee'. It is, of course, quite possible for communication to take place **without** Language – or else every means of communication would automatically be Language, hence rendering the term 'Language' intellectually vacuous; but Language cannot exist without communication being somehow involved. This inherent communicative character of Language – that is, the fact that Language is necessarily used for communication, or that Language is indeed what it is essentially because of the communication function[5] it has to serve – may be aptly illustrated as follows by comparing Language to aircraft.

The *raison d'être* of any aircraft, the purpose for which the aircraft exists, is **flight**: this is the motivating factor which causes the aircraft to be what it is; in other words, flying is the guiding principle which gives coherence to all the aircraft's parts, binding them together into a specific whole. It is truly possible to build aircraft for other purposes besides flight – including recreation, for instance; but, **by their very nature**, aircraft are designed to fly, and this purpose or function determines how they are built (in other words, determines their make-up or structure) – such that pioneers of aircraft construction sacrificed virtually every other purpose for flight; and even modern aircraft builders would readily admit that 'aircraft' built on principles which inherently (i.e. **not** accidentally) make them incapable of flying **look like** aircraft, but are **not really** aircraft, no matter how comfortable or beautiful, and so on, they may otherwise be. Furthermore, the **specialised purpose of** an aircraft, apart from the inherent general

---

5 What has just been said definitely does **not** imply that Language may not be used for other purposes besides communication.

one of flight common to all aircraft, determines the exact structure of that particular aircraft. For example, the make-up of a fighter aircraft must be such as permits not just flight generally, the characteristic of **every** aircraft, but also the **specialised** purpose of air-launched destruction of enemy targets, which is specially required of fighter aircraft.

Language, too, would still be Language even if it permitted no other function besides communication, while 'Language' whose make-up inherently made communication impossible would **not really** be Language but would **look like** Language at best, howsoever apparently useful it might be in some other respect(s): ordinary apparent 'spoken language', for instance, which necessarily does not communicate is mere noise, **not** language; the 'language' of a music piece which is devoid of communicative power is mere music, not language; and so on. Moreover, the specialised purpose of a language, apart from the general and obligatory one of communication, determines the peculiar make-up of that (kind of) language. For example, the make-up of a given poetic language must be such as to permit not just the general function of communication, which is characteristic of every language, but also the specialised function of artistic expression such as is required of poetic language.

Now, communication, the essential function of Language as I have just demonstrated, is clearly **not** part of Language – even though, as I have just demonstrated in some detail, it is an essential part of the nature of Language. It follows, then, that the structure of Language, the only serious preoccupation of Generativist Linguistics, is **insufficient** to account for the nature of Language. Whereby the failure of Generativist Linguistic

Theory, since it lacks any serious characterisation of the Language use essentials of the nature of Language.

The distinctive character of linguistic communication

It makes for a better understanding of the nature of Language to be able to distinguish clearly between Language as a means of communication and other, non-linguistic, means of communication – thus. Briefly, Language is a **representational means** of communication, while other communication tools are **indicational means** of communication.

An indicational means of communication is an **indirect** means that **implies** what is being communicated by 'pointing to' that thing. This type of communication occurs much more frequently than we usually realise in 'real world acts' – that is, in the more or less routine real-life preoccupations (such as falling asleep, carrying your suitcase, taking a walk, shooting your pistol, smoking several cigarettes, lighting a candle, sneezing, etc.) which should ordinarily constitute subjects-matter for communication, rather than pass for communicative actions themselves as such. Now, communication by indication under these circumstances is where some given state of affairs is **deduced** (i.e., reasoned out) by some observer, whom we may correctly call the communicatee here, as the logical implication of some particular real world act(s), which interpretation the performer of the act(s), whom we may correctly call the communicator here, so intended. Briefly, to indicate **a** with **b** according to this explanation of indication just presented is to make **a** the logical consequence of **b** – where **b** is a communication means, and **a** a communication intent conveyed with **b**.

19

The communication intent here, **a**, is, in other words, **implied** (i.e., **indirectly** expressed) with **b**, the communication means. We may also call the communication means here an **indicator** and the communication intent[6] the **indicated**. The relationship between an indicator and its indicated is then said to be **indicational** in this sense that an indicator points to (i.e., leads to) its corresponding indicated by logical implication; and the communicatee makes the necessary deduction (that '**b** indicates **a**') in the communication situation on a more or less *ad hoc* basis – that is, without prior obligatory learning specifying this particular interpretation as being what must apply in the communication setting.

Consider the following illustration as an example of indicational communication. As you approach a taxicab in a taxi park here in Benin City, the driver of the cab standing by it **sees you coming** towards him, studiously shuts the cab's doors, sits on a bench nearby and starts reading a newspaper with 'furious' concentration. It is quite possible to misunderstand the cab driver's intent in the context; but it does happen that his 'real world acts' (of shutting his cab's doors, sitting on a bench, reading a newspaper...) lead you to the logical conclusion that he is not for hire now. This logical conclusion (that the driver is not for hire now) is here obviously **implied** (that is indirectly expressed), and NOT specified /stated as such by the cab driver. Now, to the extent that this particular **deduction** is what the cab driver actually intended you all along to arrive at by his actions, then he has indeed communicated that intent to you indirectly – that is, by indication. According to my hypothesis in

---

6 By 'communication intent' I refer to what is communicated, **not** to the desire to communicate - which I call a communication intention.

Performative Linguistics, indication as just presented and illustrated is the **general** means of communication, which **all** communicating beings have in common, since any communicating individual can use real world acts to convey his/ her/ its intent.

Representation is the other major type of communication mode according to my hypothesis in Performative Linguistics; it is the **specialised means** of communication which only Language-using individuals have. A representational means of communication is a **direct means** that **states** what is being communicated by 'standing for' that thing. Communication by representation thus restrictively understood occurs where some particular state of affairs is **knowable by convention** by the communicating parties involved (of communicator and communicatee), but not necessarily through any kind of formally struck agreement, as the **specific referent** for some given acts. To represent **a** with **b** according to this definition is to make **b** assume the place of **a** — where again **b** is a communication means and **a** the communication intent conveyed with **b**. The communication intent here, **a**, is **stated** (i.e., **directly** expressed), NOT implied, with **b**, the communication means. We may also call the communication means here a **representer** and the communication intent its **represented**.

The relationship between the representer and its represented is **representational** in this sense that a representer **recalls** (i.e., **re-presents**) its corresponding represented by laid-down convention, and the communicatee makes the necessary recognition (that **b** represent **a**) in the communication situation concerned based on a **code** – that is, as a result of a previous obligatorily learned set of rules that stipulate some particular interpretation as being what should correctly apply in the given communication setting.

Take, for an illustrative example of communication by representation as just presented, a traffic warden's raising of his/her hand to communicate to you to stop your moving vehicle. The raising of the hand here stands for, and thus recalls, the state of affairs 'I require you to stop your vehicle' – such that when you see the warden raise his/her hand you understand precisely, based on your previously learned convention stipulating that this particular interpretation is what applies for the warden's act, the interpretation that the warden requires you to stop your moving vehicle. Accordingly, the warden's raising of his/her hand as just presented is, being a representational and communicative code, a **linguistic** means of communication. So, too, is the verbal production "Queue up!" from a shopkeeper to a customer in a supermarket, because its correct interpretation depends on the customer having previously learned the representational communicative code (called 'English') that permits him/her to identify the exact corresponding communication intent which that production should refer to.

From the above discussion, we have seen how Language may be distinguished from non-linguistic means of communication by the fact that it is essentially a **representational** communicative tool (i.e., we use Language to **assume the place** of the realities that preoccupy our consciousness, in order to share those experiences with one another as information), while non-linguistic means of communication are **indicational** communicative tools (i.e., we use them to **make inferences about** the realities that preoccupy our consciousness, in order to share those experiences with one another as information). But Language may also, incidentally, be used as an indicational phenomenon, **in**

addition to (NOT in place of) being intrinsically representational. If, for example, you tell your visitor who has been in your house too late into the night for your liking that you are feeling very sleepy, you could not only represent thereby with your language texture the state of affairs or intent that 'you are feeling very sleepy' but also indicate (i.e., by logical implication of that statement also communicate **indirectly**) that your visitor should leave your house immediately (so that you can go to bed). Language performance here, as 'a real world act' in its own right too, has become also an indicational means of communication, over and above communicating representationally by its inherent nature.

Language communication skills

Since Language is inherently a **communication** tool, knowledge of Language or Language Competence, which is indispensable for any use of Language, consists of a certain number of **communication** skills, which may therefore be called 'Language communication skills' – given that we are concerned here with linguistic communication specifically. They are 'skills' in the sense that they involve different degrees of **proficiency**, depending for instance on the inherent linguistic abilities as well as assiduity for language acquisition of the Language users concerned; they constitute knowledge we have to have in order to become Language-using communicating individuals. Language communication skills may be conveniently classified into two broad divisions – namely:

i.   intralinguistic communication skills; and

ii. extralinguistic communication skills.

Intralinguistic communication skills

Intralinguistic communication skills are communication skills of Language **texture**: they comprise what it entails to know the Language object itself, for its use to be **possible**, and are accordingly the **core** constituents of Language communication skills. Given that Language is made up of thought and symbolisation as we saw in chapter one, intralinguistic communication skills may be defined alternatively as the 'ability to construct thought structures as well as their corresponding representing symbolisation structures for the communication of experiences, and the ability to comprehend what is communicated with those two structures'. Intralinguistic communication skills may accordingly be illustrated as follows.

Linguistic construction and comprehension

Some individual, a potential Language communicator (i.e., one who knows some language for communicating thereby), impelled by some motive, has something he/she intends to communicate. For example, he/she could be impelled to communicate his/her desire to know what names HALLIDAY's initials 'M.A.K.' stand for. I call this reality or state of affairs he/she wishes to communicate an 'experience' – that is, a 'something experienced' or visualised somehow by the mind prior to communication (**not** the experiencing process or activity itself of the mind) – because the potential Language communicator's mind has first to be aware of it (in other words, to 'experience' it), before then making the communicatee also aware of it through Language. The Language so used comprises **both** the communicator's **mental image** called 'thought', representing the experienced reality I call an 'experience', **and** the form, called 'symbolisation' (which is **not necessarily** sound), representing that thought.

In modern Linguistics, an experience as presented above is sometimes also called a **referent**, the thought a **reference**, and the symbolisation of the thought a **referend**. Thus, the Language communicator's intent to know what names HALLIDAY's initials 'M.A.K.' stand for is an experience or referent, his/her mental image representing that experience is his/her thought or reference, and the form captured by the written marks below representing that thought is his/her symbolisation or referend.[7]

1. What do the initials 'M. A. K.' stand for?

The three Rs – referent, reference, and referend – of Language construction and comprehension may conveniently be designated as R_1, R_2, and R_3 respectively, strictly according to

---

[7] The terms 'referent', 'reference', and 'referend' are applicable not just to Language communication with individual sentence wholes but to the constituent lexical units and phrases of sentences for Language communication. They also apply to Language communication involving structures of Language larger than sentences.

their order of appearance for the **communicator**, as illustrated below.

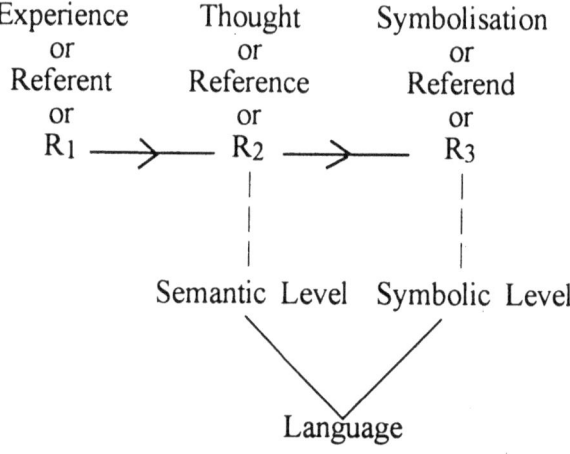

Fig. 6: *The Three Rs of Language Construction*

Communication has taken place when the communicatee 'shares' the communicator's experience, by equally becoming conscious of that same reality earlier experienced by the communicator – as follows:

(i) the communicatee receives the form or referend first;
(ii) he/she gets the referend's meaning or reference by recalling the appropriate thought that referend represents for that language community; and
(iii) he/she understands the reference's information or referent by determining the appropriate reality that thought represents for the language community in question. These

three Rs of Language comprehension,[8] in their order of appearance for the communicatee, are illustrated below.

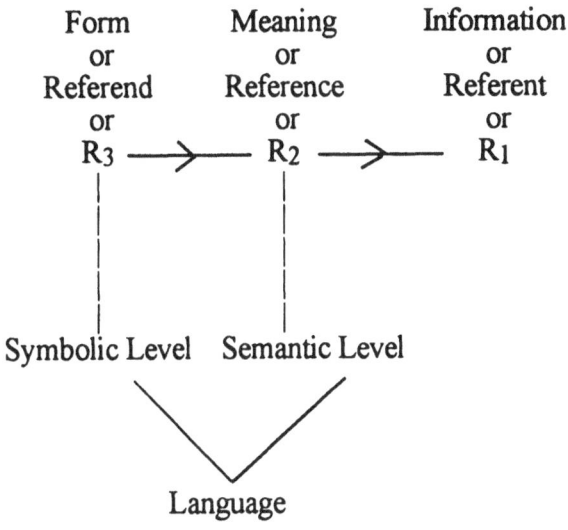

Fig. 7: *The Three Rs of Language Comprehension*

The distinctive character of representational relationships

Earlier in this chapter I distinguished Language as a means of communication from other, non-linguistic, means of communication thus: Language is a **representational** means of communication inherently, while other communication tools are

---

8 This linear and representational model of form, meaning, and reality (of the so-called "Three Rs" of referend, reference, and referent) within the Performative Linguistics paradigm purports to constitute a very significant improvement upon the traditional triangular model of concepts, forms, and things - as in OGDEN and RICHARDS (1923).

essentially **indicational** means of communication. From my illustrations just presented above of Language construction and Language comprehension, it should be clear that not only is Language as a whole inherently representational with respect to the experiences/information or R_1 it conveys but also that the thought/meaning or R_2 immediate constituent of Language is representational with respect to the said experiences/information or R_1, while the symbolisation/form or R_3 immediate constituent of Language is representational with respect to the thought/meaning or R_2 part of Language. For a better understanding of the nature of Language content, knowledge of which constituents constitutes intralinguistic skills, let me now expatiate on this representational relationship between the three R_S.

A **representational** relationship, it should be immediately emphasised, does **not** necessarily imply any **resemblance** between the representer and the represented. For example, the present (i.e., in the year 2002) President of Nigeria, Chief Olusegun OBASANJO, delegates a member of his government to **represent** him at a Commonwealth of Nations meeting in London; his representer does **not** have to be an ex-army General like himself the represented, and does **not** have to be male either like himself; all that matters in the situation is that by common agreement of all parties concerned it be understood that the person chosen by the President of Nigeria should assume the President's position (i.e., should stand for the President) – such that whatever that representer says officially at the said meeting in his/her capacity as the President's representer, regarding the position of Nigeria on a pertinent issue discussed, it should be assumed to be what the represented, Chief OBASANJO himself, says is the position of Nigeria on that issue. Similarly, the relationship between the thought and symbolisation (i.e., between the 'meaning' and 'form') components of Language is such that there is **not necessarily** any resemblance between the thought, the represented, and the symbolisation, the representer.

Since antiquity in ancient Indian linguistic scholarship, and especially with the teachings of the famous Swiss Linguist, Ferdinand de SAUSSURE, at the beginning of the twentieth century, the above observation about Language has been expressed by many Language scholars in these terms, that "the relationship between a Language form and its meaning is (essentially) arbitrary". But this formulation is only **partially** correct, since, although the overwhelming majority of Language forms may indeed have the so-called "arbitrary" relationship with their corresponding meanings, there is nothing arbitrary about the relationship between an onomatopoeia (like 'zoom' being the word for the sound made by a car taking off) as a Language form and its corresponding meaning (here, in the example of the word 'zoom', what we English speakers think the car taking off sounds like – "Zoo – oo – m"); and dismissing summarily such cases of resemblance between Language form and Language meaning as mere "exceptions" simply begs the question; for we are still left with the glaring fact that **not all** Language forms do entertain an "arbitrary" relationship with their corresponding Language meanings.

Now, my position on the matter in Performative Linguistics is to consider the relationship between a representer and its represented to be 'neutral' – that is, **neither necessarily** "arbitrary" (i.e., non-resembling), **nor necessarily** "natural" (i.e., resembling). Thus, in the case of Chief Olusegun OBASANJO presented earlier, it is **irrelevant** (hence, a 'neutral' case) whether that Chief OBASANJO's representer does resemble him or not; what matters is that it be understood by all concerned that the representer does stand for him, Chief OBASANJO, the represented. In any given case of representation, the representer of Chief OBASANJO will of course either resemble him or not resemble him; but, in principle, it does not matter which of the two alternatives is actually the case. So, too, with Language: it is irrelevant (hence, a 'neutral' case) whether referends (i.e., symbolisations, called 'forms' usually) resemble or do not resemble references (i.e., thoughts – called 'meanings' usually); for Language would still conceivably be Language if no resemblance existed at all between referends and references, or if resemblance happened somehow to exist in all cases between referends and references; what matters is that such and such referends do stand for such and such references by common agreement.

Furthermore, according to Performative Linguistics theory in the matter, the relationship between references (i.e., thoughts or 'meanings') and referents (i.e., realities, which I call 'experiences') is also "neutral" – that is, it is irrelevant also whether Language thoughts are true mental pictures of the realities they represent, or not true mental pictures of those realities; what matters is that by convention[9] of a language community's members concerned those thoughts do identify and

---

[9] The mental pictures of experienced realities peculiar to a given language community are 'conventional' in the sense that they are **habitual** characteristic strategies of the given language community for making sense of realities, and hence for communicating them. As such, the strategies are neither necessarily true nor necessarily false characterisations of realities, but are, like any other cultural constructs, just social artifacts convenient for the community. It follows that for any two given language communities, the world picture (i.e., the global mental imaging of reality) of one cannot reasonably be said to be better or worse than another - simply **different.**

recall specific entities or states of affairs, and not others, for intercommunication between members of the given language community. For example, the state of affairs which members of the English language community visualise mentally in terms of 'the sun has set' is differently conceived mentally by the Igbo, Bini, and French language communities with 'the sun has fallen', 'the sun has fallen into the sea/ocean', and 'the sun has lain down' – to communicate **the same** natural phenomenon ostensibly.

We shall appreciate later in this book the real importance for Linguistics of the foregoing clarifications about the representational nature of Language's two immediate constituents. For now, let us continue with the general characterisation of intralinguistic communication skills.

Active Language Competence and Passive Language Competence

I reiterate for the discussion that intralinguistic communication skills comprise two main kinds of abilities: (i) the ability to be a communicator using Language by producing texts[10] of a language for others to interpret; and (ii) the ability to be a communicatee using the same language by being able to understand texts of that language produced by others for him/her to interpret. The Language communicator's ability to produce texts of a language is generally called an '**active** language competence' (or an **active competence** for short), while the Language

---

10 'Text' in current Linguistics is the technical term for a communicative Language construct - whether it is written, spoken, or gestural.

31

communicatee's ability to understand texts produced for him/her to interpret is usually called a '**passive** language competence' (or a **passive competence** for short).

The communicator's type of Language competence is called 'active' because Language communication is essentially **performed** by the communicator (not the communicatee) and the communicatee's role is 'passive' in the sense that it is like that of an intelligent observer (of the communicator's performance), who has to put himself/herself in the communicator's place to be able to comprehend the communicator's Language performance. From the just-stated fact about the inherent nature of Language communication, it follows that **a theory of Language as it is used in real-life situations must be communicator-centred.**

Because it is inherently more difficult to construct texts than to comprehend them, all Language users tend to be better at understanding the texts of any language they know than at producing the texts of that language: we all tend to understand the sentences of any language we know better than we ourselves can produce them in communication. In other words, our **active** competence (i.e., our ability to construct texts of a given language) is as a rule **weaker** than our corresponding passive competence (i.e., our ability to comprehend the texts of a given language) for any language we know. However, the difference between the active competence and the passive competence is not usually significant enough to be easily noticed for a language we know well, like our first language usually; and, in that case, it is said that the individual concerned has a (very) "good" or "strong" active competence of that language. Sometimes, though, especially when it comes to mastering a second language after puberty, the difference between active competence and passive competence, even when the individual concerned has a reasonable fluency level for the language in question, may be much more readily noticeable.[11] You may then sometimes hear such a person admit: "Oh, I have no problem at all understanding that language; it is just that I don't speak or write it easily". In this specific type of case, it is said that the person has an essentially **passive** language competence (or, in short, a **passive competence**) of the language in question. It goes without saying that since a strong active competence normally implies a strong passive competence too (but **not** vice versa), Language teachers in general should emphasise the acquisition of a good active competence by their students/pupils; and that, also, all translators should possess a very good active competence of their working target languages.

Extralinguistic communication skills

We recall that to know any language – that is, to have a linguistic competence – is to have acquired certain specific communication skills, since Language is inherently a communication tool, and that these skills may be classified into **two** broad divisions: (i) **intra**linguistic communication skills, which I have just discussed at some length, and (ii) **extra**linguistic communication skills, which I shall now proceed to elucidate.

---

11 This explains well why interviewed professional translators are ever so often required to specify their working 'target language(s)' - i.e., the languages they can readily **construct** texts of for translating the texts of some other language(s) they also know.

While intralinguistic communication skills are skills of Language **text**, extralinguistic communication skills are skills of Language **context**: they comprise what it entails to know how to use the Language object for that use to be **appropriate**, and are thus the **peripheral** constituents of Language communication skills – as opposed to intralinguistic communication skills which we have seen to be the **core** constituents of Language communication skills, since they concern Language texture or content itself. Extralinguistic communication skills may also be described as the modalities or conditions for communication with Language to be suitable; and they consist of **two** basic constituents:
(i) the **general** skills; and
(ii) the **specific** skills.

General extralinguistic communication skills concern the knowledge of 'world' realities that are the possible subjects-matter for Language communication generally, and which comprise the communicable preoccupations of the Language-using individuals as existent members of a language community. The 'world' realities of general extralinguistic communication skills may also be defined as the 'social context' or 'remote context' for language communication – which must be known for the use of Language to be appropriate.

These realities consist therefore not only of physical and biological phenomena such as rivers and plants respectively, as they are experienced by members of a given language community, but also the culture of their language community – that is, the total body of material artifacts (such as tools, weapons, houses, etc.), of mental artifacts (such as beliefs, values, aesthetic perceptions, etc.), and of behavioural artifacts of distinctive forms of behaviour (such as rituals, modes of dress, greetings, etc.) created by the community (sometimes deliberately, sometimes through unforeseen circumstances beyond that community's control), and (though undergoing kinds and degrees of changes continuously) transmitted from generation to generation through non-biological means (that is, through learning).[12]

Specific extralinguistic communication skills concern knowledge of contextual factors that are the typical constraints on the communicator for specific Language communication acts, and comprise the actual (typical) circumstances for the Language-using individual's Language **choices** in communication as an integral member of a particular language community. The 'contextual factors' of specific extralinguistic communication skills may also be described as the 'psychological context', or the 'immediate context', of Language communication – which must be known for the chosen texture of Language in Language use to be suitable. In Performative Linguistics, the contextual factors are usually designated simply as **the** (extralinguistic) communication context for Language performance – 'communication context', for short. These are seven in number, according to my hypothesis – that is, **the** 'communication context' for Language use may be described as a complex comprising seven contingent factors. These factors are called "variables" (i.e., 'Language communication context variables') in Performative Linguistics, since they **vary** in manifestation and import according to the exact Language communication acts under consideration. They are presented as follows.

---

12 See BULLOCK, A. and STALLYBRASS, O. (eds. 1977:150) from where this definition is derived.

	Variables	Target
LANGUAGE	Who?	The communicator of the information
	What?	The subject matter of the information
	Why?	The reason for transmitting the information
COMMUNICATION	Where?	The location for transmitting the information
	When?	The occasion, including pertinent events, of the information transmission
CONTEXT	Which?	The medium for transmitting the information
	Whom?	The communicatee of the information transmission

Fig. 8: The Psychological or Immediate Context of Language Communication

Linguistic Competence and Linguistics

To conclude our discussion in this chapter, it has been noted that linguistic competence or knowledge of Language is **NOT just** a matter of Language structure, as in Generative Grammar:

it consists of **both** the structural **and** the use essential constituents of the nature of Language – viz, (i) intralinguistic competence or textual linguistic competence (concerning the knowledge of Language **texture** itself), and (ii) extralinguistic competence or contextual linguistic competence (concerning the knowledge of Language **contexture**). Briefly put, linguistic competence, or the knowledge of Language, involves **more** than the knowledge of Language structure features, the sole preoccupation of Generative Grammar, to include the knowledge of Language use particularities also as understood in Performative Linguistics.

Now, if the goal of Linguistics as a science is to characterise Language in its entire nature, then Linguistics may also be divisible into the following two main sub-disciplines of scientific study:

(i) Language Structure Linguistics or Textual Linguistics, usually called 'Grammar', and

(ii) Language Use Linguistics or Contextual Linguistics, usually called 'Pragmatics'.

LINGUISTICS

Structural Linguistics	Use Linguistics
Language Structure Linguistics or Textual Linguistics	Language Use Linguistics or Contextual Linguistics
Grammar	**Pragmatics**

Fig. 9: Linguistics = Grammar + Pragmatics

CHAPTER 3

SEMANTICS AND GRAMMAR

Grammar = Structural Semantics + Structural Symbolics

Another inherent flaw in Generative Grammar's syntacticist characterisation of Language I now wish to examine in some detail is the erroneous assumption that **the whole of** the study of Language meaning, Semantics, is part of the study of Language structure, Grammar – thus:

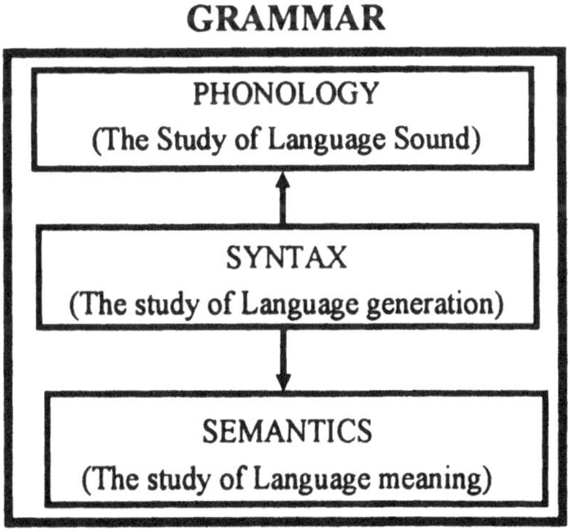

GRAMMAR

```
┌─────────────────────────────────┐
│         PHONOLOGY               │
│  (The Study of Language Sound)  │
└─────────────────────────────────┘
                ↕
┌─────────────────────────────────┐
│          SYNTAX                 │
│ (The study of Language generation)│
└─────────────────────────────────┘
                ↕
┌─────────────────────────────────┐
│         SEMANTICS               │
│ (The study of Language meaning) │
└─────────────────────────────────┘
```

Fig. 1: Grammar, the Study of Language Structure, According to Generative Grammar

As pointed out in chapter one of this book, however, if we consider Language content to be made up essentially of **both** thought (or 'meaning') **and** symbolisation (or 'form') **only**, then Linguistics, the scientific study of Language, may accordingly also be divided into two main parts with respect to that Language content – viz, (i) Semantics, the scientific study of Language thought or meaning; and (ii) Symbolics, the scientific study of Language symbolisation or form:

LINGUISTICS (the scientific study of Language)

SYMBOLICS the scientific study of symbolisation/'form'
SEMANTICS the scientific study of thought/'meaning'

Fig. 5: Linguistics = Semantics + Symbolics

What this amounts to is that Semantics covers **all** types of the study of thought (**not just** those concerning the structure of thought). Also, correspondingly, Symbolics covers **all** types of the study of symbolisation (**not just** those concerning the **structure** of symbolisation).

Thus, the error that the **whole** of the study of Language thought or 'meaning' is part of Grammar derives from the fact that, in their fascination for Language structure, Generative Grammarians do **not** seem to realise that the thought or 'meaning' component of Language may also be studied in non-structural terms – apart from being studied structurally of course. For example, the extent to which the mental constructs we call thoughts (or 'meanings') of given language communities correspond to the communities members' **understanding** of 'the world' or 'Reality', which we shall examine at some length in this chapter, contributes significantly to elucidating the nature of thought/'meaning', but is nevertheless **non**-structural in its essence as just presented. Similarly, the symbolisation or 'form' constituent of Language may also be studied in **non**-structural terms, besides being studied in structural terms of course. For example, the sounds of spoken Language – a type of symbolisation – may be studied in terms of how they are produced with articulatory organs; and these are **non**-structural studies as just presented, which do nevertheless have significant implications for our knowledge about the nature of Language sounds.

What the above discussion amounts to is this: that we may describe Grammar, the study of Language structure, to be concerned only with the **structural** aspects of the two and only two major constituents of Language – i.e, with the structural aspects of thought or 'meaning', and with the structural aspects of symbolisation or 'form' in the study of Language. In other words, Grammar is no more and no less than Structural (or Textual) Semantics, the study of the structure of Language thought or 'meaning', **plus** Structural (or Textual) Symbolics, the study of the structure of Language symbolisation or 'form'.

GRAMMAR (the study of Language structure)

Structural or Textual Symbolics
Structural or Textual Semantics

Fig. 10: Grammar = Textual Semantics + Textual Symbolics

Contextual Semantics is NOT part of Grammar

Similarly, following the insights provided by fig. 9 at the end of Chapter Two, we may also describe Pragmatics to be no more and no less than **Use** (or Contextual) Semantics plus **Use** (or Contextual) Symbolics:

PRAGMATICS (the study of Language use)

Use or Contextual Symbolics
Use or Contextual Semantics

Fig. 11: Pragmatics = Contextual Semantics + Contextual Symbolics

Now, putting together, for greater clarity, the contents of figs 10 and 11, which derive from the contents of figs 5 and 9, to make up Linguistics as a whole, we see that Linguistics thus comprises Structural or Textual Semantics plus Use or Contextual Semantics on the one hand, and Structural or Textual Symbolics plus Use or Contextual Symbolics on the other hand, as follows:

LINGUISTICS (the scientific study of Language)

Symbolics	Structural or Textual Symbolics	Use or Contextual Symbolics
Semantics	Structural or Textual Semantics	Use or Contextual Semantics
	Grammar	Pragmatics

Fig. 12: Linguistics = Textual Semantics and Contextual Semantics + Textual Symbolics and Contextual Symbolics

Next, relating Semantics to Grammar, based on fig. 12 above, we see clearly that **only part of Semantics is part of Grammar** – precisely, Textual (or Structural) Semantics. **Contextual (or Use) Semantics is definitely NOT part of Grammar** – which is a fact of tremendous intellectual importance completely missed by the syntacticist Linguistics of Generative Grammar.

The domain of Semantics

How should Semantics be further constituted in Linguistics as a whole, where it features as one of the two major components of the science discipline? Within Linguistics, Semantics may, first of all, be further subcategorised into:

(i) **Conceptual Semantics**, the study of the fundamental units of thought, called 'concepts', and

(ii) **Propositional Semantics**, all study of the supra-conceptual units of Language thought, called 'propositions' in Performative Linguistics.

There is, furthermore, a third, sub-conceptual, constituent of Semantics, **Nuclear Semantics**, which is the study of the ultimate Language thought elements called 'semantic particles', from which concepts are created. Nuclear Semantics, Conceptual Semantics, or Propositional Semantics may of course be conducted structurally or/and non-structurally. Therefore, it is Structural (or Textual) Nuclear Semantics, Structural (or Textual) Conceptual Semantics, and Structural (or Textual) Propositional Semantics that are parts of Grammar. Use (or Contextual) Nuclear Semantics, Use (or Contextual) Conceptual Semantics, and Use (or Contextual) Propositional Semantics are parts of Pragmatics.

Let us now propose a sample illustrative demonstration of the content of the various constituents of Semantics in Linguistics. Let us begin with Conceptual Semantics.

Conceptual Semantics

The subject matter of Conceptual Semantics is the concept, and the goal of Conceptual Semantics is therefore Conceptual Theory – the theory of the concept. Thus, the preoccupation of Conceptual Semantics as a subscience of Linguistics is the nature of the concept; i.e., what the concept is.

What is a 'concept'?

A 'concept' refers technically to the 'idea' (i.e., mental image)[1] of any object whatsoever – whether concrete or abstract, animate or inanimate, existing or imaginary – which idea is communicated with some conventional name used to designate it. Thus, the word 'clock' is in effect a conventional name whose usage conjures up in our minds, as members of the English language community, the idea of some physical object in reality quite distinct from the idea of it in our minds; and this idea which is recallable through the use of the conventional name 'clock' is what is called a 'concept', the meaning of the word 'clock'. Similarly, there is the concept of some abstract object which the word 'virtue' calls up in our minds, and the

---

1. As I pointed out when discussing the representational nature of Language in Chapter Two, the image is **not necessarily** a true or an accurate picture of the object or reality it designates: all that matters is that we do know what object or reality the idea refers to. This means that for a fundamental unit of Language (i.e., for a 'sign' or 'lexical item') which is therefore made up of **both** a fundamental thought unit **and** a fundamental form unit, the relationship between an object and its idea or mental image is just as **representational** as that between the idea and the word used to name it - where the question of resemblance is **irrelevant**.

concept of an imaginary person which the word 'Rambo' evokes in our minds; etc.

Following the definition of 'concept' provided above, the idea of past time abstraction which is communicated with the postfix conventional name '-ed' is a concept; so, too, is the idea of an activity, that is also a concept, which the word 'dance' itself stands for:

1. Annette and Eva danced gracefully

Incidentally, we can see from the above illustration that a concept may not only be simplex, like the past time concept represented by the '-ed' affix of the word 'dance' above, or the activity concept represented by the word 'dance' itself (in each of which examples the concept is composed of only one concept), but also sometimes be complex, like the whole concept represented by the word 'danced' above (in which example the whole concept is indeed made up of **two** simple concepts).

Also following the definition of 'concept' in this chapter, any idea for which there is no conventional name to convey it within a word is not a concept. Thus, the ideas of:

(i) dying,

(ii) loss of air,

(iii) liquid,

that are associable with the word 'drown' in sentence example 2 below are **not** concepts with reference to that word 'drown', because there are no forms in that word ''drown'' which individually name each of those ideas; rather, those several ideas in fact collectively constitute what we know to be the concept which that word 'drown' calls up in our minds with as its conventional name.[2]

2. Ducks don't drown in water

These and all other ideas-constituents of concepts which are **unnamed in** the words representing the concepts are called **semantic particles** – the subject matter of Nuclear Semantics.

Other ideas for which there are no formal means of representation may be thus unnamed essentially because they are unique to the sentient object who has them, are **not** characteristic of social groupings therefore, and are thus virtually incommunicable even indirectly. Such ideas, too, are **not** concepts.

Conceptual indeterminacy

Even the native user of any given language finds himself/herself often incapable really of specifying, when so required, exactly which concept is involved with regard to a particular symbolic representer. Earlier in this chapter we were able to identify the concept represented by '— ed' of the word 'danced' in sentence example I as that of 'past time' abstraction.

---

2. In other words, the idea of drowning is made up of those of (i) dying, (ii) loss of air, and (iii) liquid: to drown is in effect to die from loss of air in some liquid.

1. Annette and Eva danced gracefully.

But consider, for illustration, another English linguistic form '-ness' – as in the English words **laziness, consciousness, friendliness, fondness**, etc.; what exactly is the concept it (i. e., '-ness') signifies? Furthermore, our linguistic intuition as members of the English language community assures us that there is some **similarity** between the concept conveyed with '-ness' as in the English words listed above on the one hand, and, on the other hand, the concept represented by each of the forms '-y' as in **discovery**, '-ty' as in **nicety**, '-ity' as in **oddity**, '-ance' as in **disturbance,** '-ism' as in **socialism**, '-ence' as in **interference**, etc.; but what exactly is the nature of that 'similarity'? Notably, do the various forms all convey one invariant concept? Or are there several related concepts involved? If the latter, what is the nature of the relationship between the several concepts? Such problems of conceptual specification because of the inherent abstract nature of the concepts involved is called **conceptual indeterminacy**.

One simplistic way out of the problem I have just sketched and named is to summarily declare that the difficulties encountered point to the hollowness of any conceptual theory in Semantics and that the various forms concerned (i.e.,'— ence', '— ance', '—ness', etc.) therefore represent **no** concept(s) as such. This kind of solution is definitely unsatisfactory, since the forms concerned do have meanings; and while we may be unable to specify those meanings accurately, it is precisely the meanings, and nothing else, that are called 'concepts': as everyone reasonably proficient in the use of English knows, the two words 'conscious' and 'consciousness', for example, differ in form from one another by only the unit 'ness', which unit must therefore be held responsible for the difference in meaning that we know as members of the English language community actually exists between 'conscious' and 'consciousness' – that is, 'ness' must somehow be meaningful for there to exist the added meaning we find represented by the word 'consciousness' where it occurs, which added meaning the word 'conscious' alone does not have. Arguments similar to that just advanced in this paragraph for the form 'ness' could be made also to affirm the meaningfulness of other form units such as 'ance', 'ence', 'ity', etc. in this discussion about conceptual indeterminacy.

My suggestion as regards the problem of conceptual indeterminacy is that Linguists should be trained to sharpen their semantic intuition through serious practice at concepts determination for the languages they know, as well as through comparison of notes with peers on their observations, difficulties, and discoveries. The findings of Semanticists already available in Philosophy and Linguistics should have been especially useful in the domain under discussion. Unfortunately, what has been discovered there to date is not much use as a help in concepts specification. The inherently abstract nature of thought makes this subject matter of Semantics largely unamenable to the application of the traditional type of practical direct-observation approach of scientific method used to date for the symbolisation level of Language – with the overall dismal result that whereas definite facts abound in such more concrete linguistic areas as Syntax, Morphology, Phonology, and Phonetics, even the delimitation of the preoccupation itself of Semantics (as distinct from, say, that of Pragmatics) is still subject to fierce intellectual debate. Briefly, a lot more of productive work needs to be done in every branch of Semantics.

Contrastive Conceptual Semantics

A very important method for the study of concepts is to contrast the concepts of different languages with one another. This is a very useful procedure since it compels us to become aware of interesting features of the concepts of our own languages which we would otherwise miss because we have become so accustomed to them that we may unconsciously treat them as universals, forgetting that they are only typical of our languages. The subdiscipline of Semantics involved with such studies just highlighted is called Contrastive Conceptual Semantics.

Conceptual inconstancy

One major observation which should immediately occur to us when we contrast languages conceptually with one another is that concepts are **not really** the same across languages. This is of course **not** to claim that no two languages ever have some concepts in common; what is being stressed here is simply that concepts are **usually** different for any given pair of languages, and that even when specific concepts of different languages are apparently identical, they are generally **not** exactly the same as they might at first have appeared to the unwary Language scholar. This **normal** difference between the concepts of languages is what may be called **conceptual inconstancy**.

The most obvious manifestation of this inconstancy is where the source language (SL) of the contrastive study has some concept which the target language (TL) does not have; or vice versa. Examples are the concepts designated by the English words 'computer' and 'hovercraft', which the Nigerian language called 'Igbo' does **not** have. Also, the concept designated by the English word 'lose' as in a match is absent from the Onicha-Ugbo dialect of Igbo which I know well – such that the information expressed with the English sentence example 3 below must at best be expressed by the Onicha-Ugbo Igbo in the roundabout way translatable to English freely as sentence example 4 below.

3. We lost a match.

4. They beat us in a match.

As earlier indicated, conceptual inconstancy between a TL and an SL may occur because the SL and TL have similar concepts which the unwary Language scholar erroneously assumes to be exactly the same. Now, the first underlying basis for such error is that the SL concepts concerned are in fact somewhat 'broader' in scope of content than the corresponding TL concepts assumed to be exactly the same as they are. Take the O/ọ[3] pronominal unit of Igbo, as in:

---

3. Which of the two (that is, whether 0 or Ọ) applies depends on the so-called rules of **vowel harmony** of Igbo : 0 will go immediately with a subsequent co-textual syllable containing any of the Igbo vowel phonemes /i/, /u/, /o/, /e/, and /ẹ/; Ọ will go immediately with a subsequent co-textual syllable containing any of the Igbo vowel phonemes /ị/,/ụ /, / ọ /, and /a/.

5. Ọjụ.

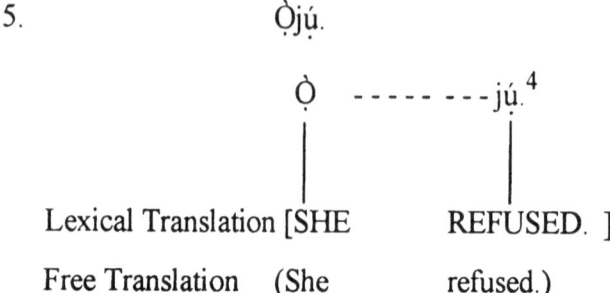

Lexical Translation [SHE   REFUSED.]
Free Translation   (She   refused.)

According to the above illustration, I have translated the Igbo[5] pronominal unit Ọ there lexically with SHE; but, actually, the pronominal unit could also be translated with HE or IT, depending on who/what is being referred to in the communication context. This amounts to saying that the Igbo o/Ọ pronominal unit concept subsumes, and is hence much broader in content than, the individual concepts of the English **he, she**, or **it**.[6]

---

4. For translation conventions used here and their underlying theoretical justifications, see UWAJEH (1993a, 1994, 1996b, 1996c, 1996d, 1999, 2001a, 2001b, and 2002).

5. The reference dialect of Igbo of my examples is that of Onicha-Ugbo in Delta State, Nigeria.

6. In this and all other pertinent examples of conceptual inconstancy for similar concepts, I am not concerned with so-called 'homonyms' (i.e, cases of several words or morphemes with exactly the same form — written and spoken) or 'polysemy' (i.e, cases of one word or morpheme with several meanings): there are not, for instance, several morphemes of Igbo with the common form O/ Ọ (one of which morphemes would thus supposedly have the same meaning as the English he, the other as the English she, and the third as the English it), nor does the form O/ Ọ call up for the Igbo three different concepts (thereby supposedly making it a form having three different meanings). No, for the above examples, used for discussing conceptual inconstancy with regard to similar concepts of SL and TL, I am stating categorically that the Igbo O/O pronominal

The type of linguistic competence difficulty highlighted with the Igbo translated sentence above is apparently the source of certain **semantic interferences** found in Language use arising from contacts between English and many indigenous Nigerian languages – for example, as reflected in the Language performance of those Nigerian pupils who could be overheard telling their classmates: "Please borrow me your pen," (instead of "Please, **lend** me your pen,"). The interference in this specific instance derives from the fact that the concept involved in the lexicon of the particular Nigerian languages concerned is neither exactly the same as that of [BORROW] nor the same as that of [LEND] in the English lexicon, but encompasses both concepts,[7] – which can only be distinguished by **contextual** facts of Language use.

Still with regard to conceptual inconstancy, similar concepts of SL and TL may in actual fact differ also because the SL concepts are 'narrower' in scope of content than the corresponding TL concepts they are assumed to be exactly the same as. Consider, for illustration, the English lexical unit '(to) shine'; it is used, rather too broadly vis-à-vis what

---

form, for instance, represents only one conceptual unit for the Igbo which is unmarked (that is, does not inherently specify) as to whether we are referring to a he , a she, or an it - just as the one English conceptual unit represented by the form it is inherently unmarked about gender.

7   From my observation of the English language performance of Danes during my visit of their country in 1993, I was able to infer that Danish, too, has a concept which is broader than either that of the English [LEND] or that of the English [BORROW], and which subsumes both of these two concepts of English - such that with Danish the context of Language communication presumably, not the lexical unit by itself, will direct the communicatee to know whether the Language communicator is concerned with a "lending" or a "borrowing" in the English language community's sense.

53

obtains for Igbo, to subsume several different concepts which the Igbo language community would specify variegatedly as follows:

(i) ínwū (for the shining of lamps, fire, and such-like objects);

(ii) ítī (for the 'shining' characteristic of the moon); and

(iii) ịmụ̀ (for the sun's typical brand of 'shining').

Propositional Semantics

Propositional Semantics is the third, highest, level of Semantics; it subsumes Conceptual Semantics and Nuclear Semantics. Propositional Semantics is further sub-categorisable into the following three major constituents of Semantics: Phrase-Thought Semantics, which studies the meanings of phrase forms; (ii) Sentence–Thought Semantics, which studies the meanings of sentences; and (iii) Text-Thought Semantics, which studies the meanings-content of Language units higher than the sentence. The different levels of Semantics mentioned in this paragraph are cumulative in the sense that: (a) Nuclear Semantics is subsumed in Conceptual Semantics, while Conceptual Semantics is subsumed in Propositional Semantics; (b) within Propositional Semantics, Phrase–Thought Semantics is subsumed in Sentence–Thought Semantics, while Sentence–Thought Semantics is in turn subsumed in Text–Thought Semantics. The just-mentioned comprehensive picture of Semantics may be displayed in the following diagrams.

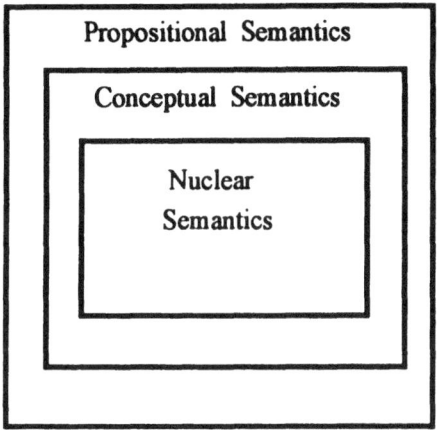

Fig. 13a: The Sub-Disciplines of Semantics, I.

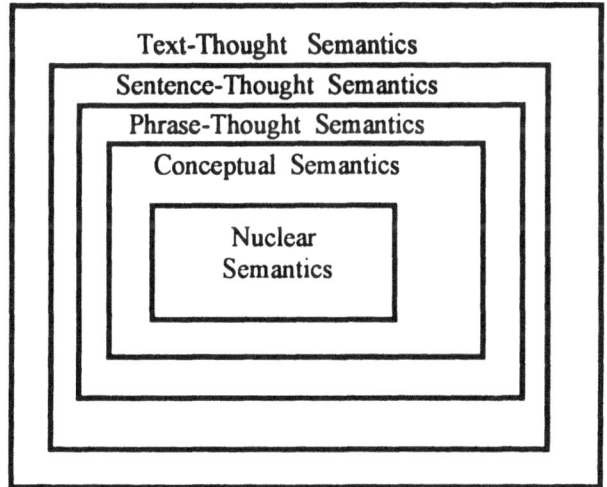

Fig. 13b: The Sub-Disciplines of Semantics, II.

The subject matter of Propositional Semantics is the **proposition**, and the goal of Propositional Semantics is therefore Propositional Theory – the theory of the proposition. Thus, the preoccupation of Propositional Semantics is the nature of the proposition, the characterisation of the proposition.

What is a 'proposition'?

In Performative Linguistics usage, a 'proposition' is any thought unit larger than the concept. Propositions are made up of concepts, since concepts are the basic or fundamental units of thought. In Language, concepts are the semantic (i.e, meaning) components of lexical units; correspondingly, propositions are the semantic constituents of phrasal units, clausal/sentential constructs, and of all other textual wholes higher than the sentence. In short, a proposition is the meaning part of any Language unit more complex than a lexical item.

Contrastive Propositional Semantics

Like Contrastive Conceptual Semantics, Contrastive Propositional Semantics – the subdiscipline of Semantics concerned with studying the differences between propositions of different languages – is very useful for drawing our attention to the features of thought of a particular language which we might otherwise miss because we have become too used to them to notice their significance. And because propositions of particular languages are in effect **thought patterns** of those languages, the more contrasts of propositions of languages we are able to conduct the better we are therefore at appreciating **the ways of structuring ideas into thought complexes** which members of different language communities exhibit with their languages.

Such contrastive semantic studies become **inevitable** when we wish to communicate with our own language, to fellow users of the language, significant grammatical particularities of some other language(s). Here, suitable **literal translations** of the texts of the described language are **obligatory**. For example, even with English lexical and free translations of the sentence example 6 presented below, an English communicator's grammatical statement that this sentence construct of UL[8] is **subjectless**, or that the equivalent UL unit for 'I' in the corresponding English free text is in fact a **locative**, can neither really be understood nor appreciated by the English language communicatee for whom UL is being described with English.

6.   Amulu   hihuso   maru.

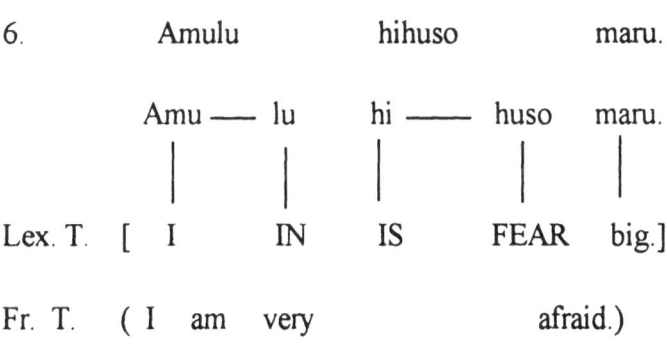

Lex. T. [I   IN   IS   FEAR   big.]

Fr. T. (I   am   very   afraid.)

---

8. 'UL', acronym for the 'Unknown Language', is used for a presumably natural language for which I have accidentally had some useful data for many years now, but whose real name I am not yet able to ascertain.

A satisfactory literal translation of the said UL sentence, as presented below, reveals the UL community's thought pattern involved, and thus makes clear the grammatical statements mentioned earlier above.

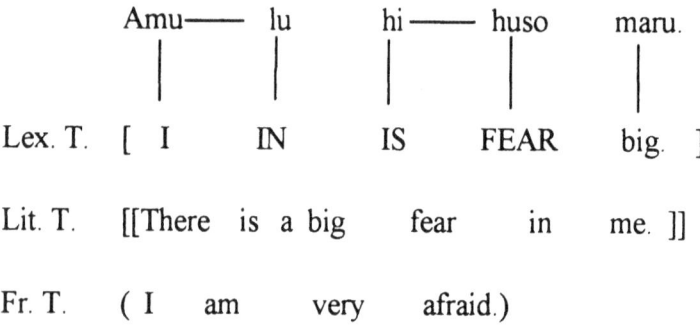

Lex. T.   [I   IN   IS   FEAR   big.]

Lit. T.   [[There is a big   fear   in   me.]]

Fr. T.   (I   am   very   afraid.)

Propositions and world picture

The thought pattern of a given language community, which a particular proposition of that Language constitutes, is no more and no less than that language community's **mental representation of reality** – i.e., a 'world picture' of that community – made manifest. Each individual proposition of the language of that community presents some specific facet of that community's world picture; and a comprehensive totality of the propositions of the language community purveys a global world picture characteristic of that given language community.

World picture as explained above is, of course, already made manifest to some degree at the conceptual level of the given community's language: there, the totality of conceptual units of the language do reveal the distinctive conventional[9] mode of **segmentation** of experienced reality, while at the propositional level a comprehensive totality of propositions of the given language reveal the characteristic conventional **reconstruction** of experienced reality – a reconstruction of which the conceptual units are constituents. Thus, for example, from the fact that in the UL community one's being afraid is ostensibly treated as a case of fear being in oneself (see sentence example 6 above where 'Amulu hihuso maru', 'I am very afraid', translates literally as 'there is a big fear in me') we capture a feature of UL community's global world picture – a characteristic mental reconstruction of reality whereby we are not surprised when told with English that for the UL community 'there is a cold in you' when you are cold, and 'there is heat in you' when you are hot; etc. And still with respect to this conventional mental representation of reality characteristic of the UL community, it may be noted for instance that the concepts of **AFRAID, COLD**, and **HOT** as states of being appear to be eloquently **absent** from the UL community's world picture.

---

9. The mental segmentation and reconstruction of experienced reality associated with concepts and propositions respectively are 'conventional' in the sense that they are **habitual** peculiar strategies of the given community for making sense of reality, and hence for communicating it. As such, the strategies are neither necessarily true nor necessarily false characterisations of reality, but are, like any other cultural constructs (that linguistic constructs are), just artifacts convenient for the community's purposes. It follows that for any two given language communities, the world picture of one cannot reasonably be said to be better or worse than another, globally speaking: simply **different**.

The SAPIR - WHORF Hypothesis revisited

Consider the following Igbo sentence for further discussion

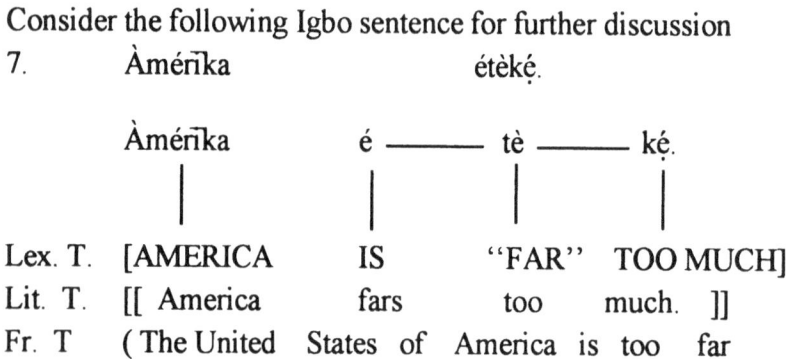

7.   Àménka   étèkẹ́.

	Àménka	é —— tè —— kẹ́.		
Lex. T.	[AMERICA	IS	"FAR"	TOO MUCH]
Lit. T.	[[America	fars	too	much.]]
Fr. T	(The United away.)	States of	America is	too far

With respect to the conceptual level of a language community's world picture, the type of question, which would sometimes be asked by non-Igbo people, is:
"Do the Igbo **really believe** that 'being far' is an **activity** which objects (like the U.S.A. in the above sentence example) may **actually perform?**". Similarly, such curious people could ask, does it follow from the fact that the Igbo language has only **three** basic concepts of colour – **WHITE, BLACK,** and **RED** – that the Igbo **really notice** in real life only the three colours conceptualised? For the propositional level of a language community's world picture, it would be asked by non-Igbo people whether one may correctly infer, for instance, from the five Igbo sentences presented below, that the Igbo language community members **actually think** that bites are bitten, cries cried, fear fears people sometimes while people fear fear at other times, and that sweetness is 'sweeted'?

8. Ńgbōàfô   tà   Ôgǒchúkwú   álụ.
   Ńgbōàfọ̀   tà   Ọ̀gǒchúkwú   álụ.
   | | | |
Lex. T. [NGBOAFO   BIT   OGOCHUKWU BITE.]
Lit. T. [[Ngboafo   bit   Ogochukwu a bite.]]
Fr. T.   (Ngboafo   bit   Ogochukwu)

9. Ọ̀gǒchúkwú   àkwá   ákwā
    Ọ̀gǒchúkwú   à _____ kwá   ákwā.
    | | | |
Lex. T. [OGOCHUKWU IS   CRY   CRY.]
Lit. T. [[Ogochukwu is   crying a cry.]]
Fr. T.   (Ogochukwu   is   crying)

10. Újō   àjọ́   Ńgbōàfọ̀.
     Újō   à _____ jọ́   Ńgbōàfọ̀.
     | | | |
Lex. T. [FEAR   IS   FEAR   NGBOAFO.
Lit. T. [[Fear is   fearing   Ngboafo.]]
Fr. T   (Ngboafo is   afraid.)

61

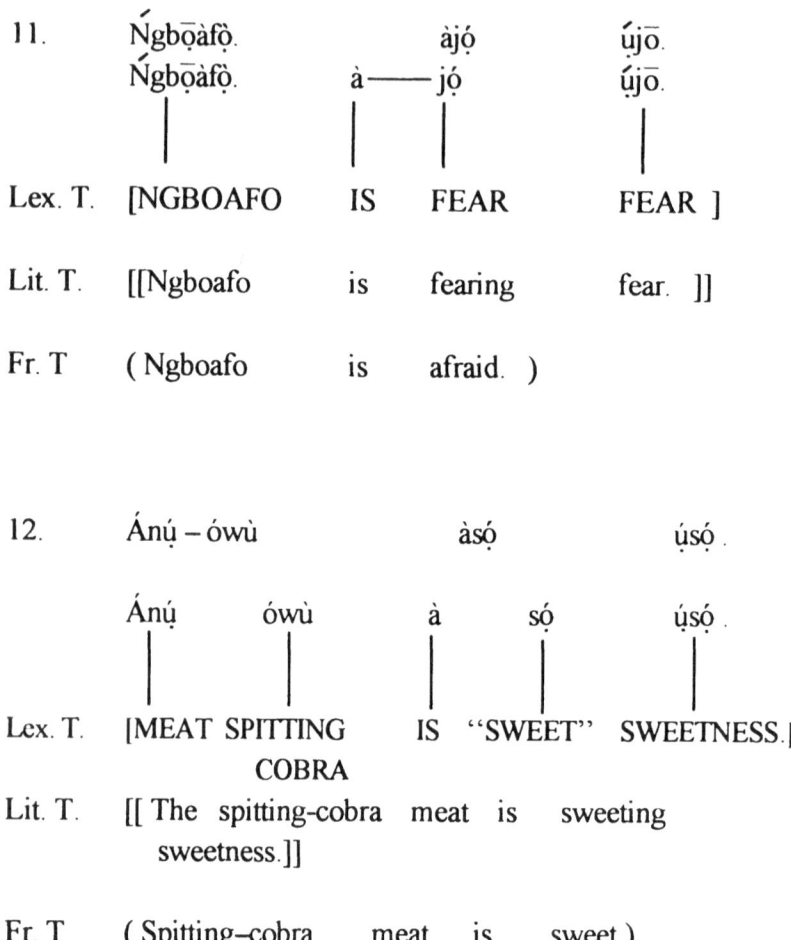

11. Ńgbōạfọ̀.   àjó   újō.
     Ńgbōạfọ̀.   à——jó   újō.
                  | | | |
Lex. T. [NGBOAFO   IS   FEAR   FEAR]

Lit. T. [[Ngboafo   is   fearing   fear.]]

Fr. T   (Ngboafo   is   afraid.)

12.   Ánụ̀ – ówù   àsọ́   ụ̀sọ́.

      Ánụ̀   ówù   à   sọ́   ụ̀sọ́.
       | | | | |
Lex. T. [MEAT SPITTING   IS   "SWEET"   SWEETNESS.]
              COBRA
Lit. T. [[The spitting-cobra meat is sweeting
              sweetness.]]

Fr. T.   (Spitting-cobra meat is sweet.)

The rationale for such questions as those listed before the above sentence examples is usually: either (i) the dread that it may indeed be the case that members of different language communities actually **understand** reality in significantly different ways just because of constraints imposed on their minds by the languages of their respective communities – in which case the strong version of the **linguistic relativity** hypothesis,[10] called **linguistic determinism**, would have been vindicated, and all sorts of weird psychoanalytic inferences may automatically be reached about every member of a given language community, based simply on the type of thought pattern manifested by that language's structure; or (ii) the fond expectation that language communities do **not** really believe, notice, or perceive, etc. according to how their languages thought patterns would have us conclude

---

10 The Linguistic Relativity (or Relativism) Hypothesis (or Theory), also called the SAPIR-WHORF Hypothesis in honour of the two American Linguists Edward SAPIR (1884 - 1939) and Benjamin Lee WHORF (1897 - 1941) reputed to be its best exponents, is the thesis that languages have special effects on the mental operations of their owners – such that each language constrains its users to manifest their thought in specific, distinct, and predictable ways quite different from those of members of another language community. Put succinctly, the hypothesis states no more and no less than that "a people's thought **pattern** is relative to that people's language"; but there is the problem of the **implication(s)** of the hypothesis, which has bedevilled its exact interpretation since it was enunciated dramatically by SAPIR and WHORF:

(i) Certain pronouncements of SAPIR and WHORF, to the effect that languages owners are **prisoners** of the thought patterns specific to their respective languages, and concerning how our perceptions are "conditioned" by the thought patterns imposed on us by our language, seem to suggest that the relativity of thought to language in question does have significant implications for how exactly we understand and deal with reality;

(ii) On the other hand, the fact that neither SAPIR nor WHORF anywhere unequivocally made the claim of determinism just alluded to, as well as the fact that tests for determinism have convincingly shown such claims to be invalid anyway, would seem to suggest that what SAPIR and WHORF really intended by their thesis about thoughts being relative to languages was simply the much more banal claim that thought patterns, or meaning structures, of language, do differ from language community to language community.

they must – in which case all that may be deduced from the apparent differences between English and Igbo thought patterns, say, in the sentence examples above, is the well-known fact that languages do differ in their meanings (as we already know they do in their forms), and there is therefore supposedly no need to make a song and dance about differences between the thought patterns of languages as if there were somehow something special about those differences.

It seems to me from my work in Performative Linguistics, concerning the linguistic relativism question being discussed in this section as it relates to the world pictures of language communities, that the correct position is neither the strong version (whereby the different thought patterns exhibited by different languages supposedly do reveal the different ways the users of those languages must **understand** reality) nor the weak version which I call **linguistic dependency** (whereby the different thought patterns exhibited by different languages are supposedly of **no** significance whatever for how owners of languages actually understand reality). To appreciate what I consider as the correct position in the matter, it is necessary to recapitulate at this juncture what I said in chapter two of this book about the **representational** nature of the relationship between Language and Reality on the one hand, then between Language thought (or 'meaning') and Language symbolisation (or 'form') on the other hand; as follows:

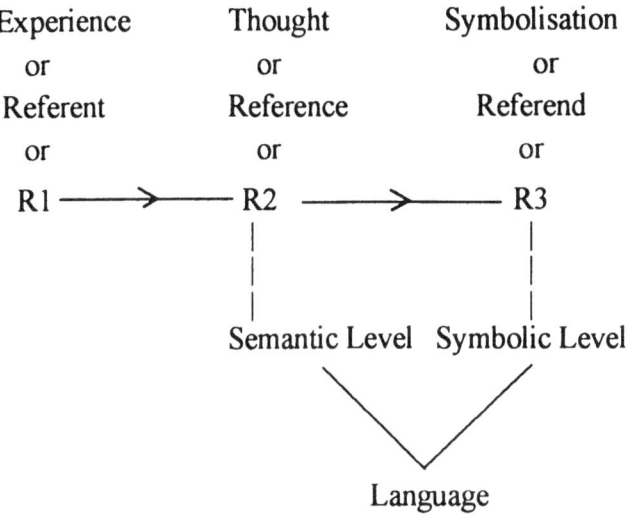

Fig. 6: The Three Rs of Language Construction

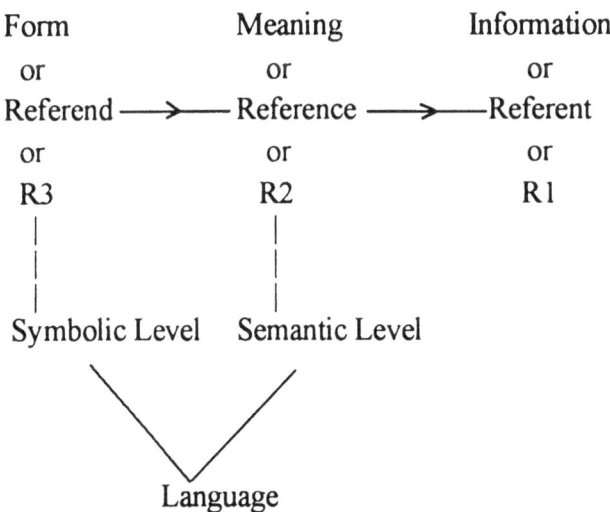

Fig. 7: The Three Rs of Language Comprehension

By its representational nature, the relationship between Language thought and reality is 'neutral', like that between Language thought and Language symbolisation – that is, it is **irrelevant** whether Language forms actually resemble the Language thoughts they stand for or not, and also **irrelevant** whether Language thoughts are really true pictures or not of the realities they 'mirror'. What matters is that it be understood by convention that such forms do stand for such thoughts and that such thoughts also stand for such realities, for communication between members of a given community. So, Language thoughts are mere **conventional pictures** constructed by each language community to stand in place of realities, and Language forms are mere **conventional media** constructed by each language community to stand in place of their thoughts of realities.

The salient point I wish to underscore here about the linguistic relativity hypothesis, however, is that a language community's specific mode of mirroring reality – i.e, the community's distinctive world picture or global thought pattern – is of great theoretical and practical significance, as follows. When you use a particular language you are automatically **bound** to picture entities and states of affairs in a specific manner, and no other, by the conventions which make you a *bona fide* member of that language community. Thus, in our Igbo language community, we must communicate about colours essentially in terms of **BLACK, WHITE** and **RED**, whatever may actually be the erudition of individual members of the Igbo language community regarding the colour spectrum – i.e., irrespective of whether individual members of the Igbo language community actually believe that there are essentially only those three colours, as some Igbo people perhaps really do, or that there are essentially more than those three colours, as many Igbo people probably do. So, too, for instance, with the state of affairs which the English conceive in terms of objects having the quality of being sweet; in the Igbo language community (see my sentence example 12 above) this state of affairs must be communicated in terms where the **quality** of being sweet does **not** exist as such, but rather objects may perform the activity of 'sweeting sweetness' (whereby they could become gustatory delights) – again, irrespective of whether or not individual members of the Igbo language community in their erudition really believe that there are such things as sweet objects, and that their sweetness actually derives from a certain quality in their state. It follows that we are indeed ''prisoners'' of the thought pattern specific to any given language in the sense **that when we use that particular language** we are automatically bound to picture entities and states of affairs in a specific manner, and no other, according to the conventions which make us *bona fide* members of that language community. It goes without saying that **no** language has **the** correct picture of the world in its inherent thought pattern; rather, each language purveys some, necessarily partial, picture of reality which (like each testimony of each spectator of a football match after the game) *ipso facto* shuts out and ignores other possibilities of picturing reality for communication.

Importance of respecting SL community's world picture

Not recognising SL community's world picture for what it is has devastating implications for the Language scholar in general, and in particular for the grammarians discussing the grammar of an SL with a TL. Consider for illustration the following Igbo sentences, with pertinent English translations provided.

13. Únọ̀kà   mà   Àdáéké   àgbàdà.
     | | | |
Lex.T. [UNOKA   PIERCED   ADAEKE   DAGGER.]
Lit. T. [[Unoka pierced   Adaeke   a dagger.]]
Fr. T. (Unoka   stabbed   Adaeke).

14. Ńgbōàfọ̀   gbà   Ọ̀gọ̌chúkwú   Ńtụ́tụ́[11]
     Ńgbōàfọ̀   gbà   Ọ̀gọ̌chúkwú   Ńtụ́tụ́.
     | | | |
Lex. T. [NGBOAFO STUNG   OGOCHUKWU   NEEDLE]
Lit. T. [[Ngboafo stung   Ogochukwu   a needle]]
Fr. T. (Ngboafo injected Ogochukwu).

11. I use a capital 'n' - i.e.; N - for writing the so-called syllabic nasal phoneme of Igbo, whose allophones manifest themselves as [ ] before posterior consonants [n] before median consonants, and [m] before anterior consonants at the beginning of pertinent words.

15. Ńgbōàfọ̀   mù   Pòlínà   Ńbọ́.
    Ńgbōàfọ̀   mù   Pòlínà   Ńbọ́.
    | | | |

Lex. T. [NGBOAFO   PINCHED   PAULINA   NAIL.]
Lit. T. [[Ngboafo   pinched   Paulina   finger nails.]]
Fr. T.   (Ngboafo   pinched   Paulina.)

16. Únòkà   gbà   éwúm   égbè.
    Únòkà   gbà   éwú —— m   égbè.
    | | | |

Lex. T. [UNOKA   SHOT   GOAT   ME   GUN]
Lit. T. [[Unoka   shot   my goat   a gun.]]
Fr. T.   (Unoka   shot   my   goat.)

17. Pòlínà   gbà   Ńkítém   úkwú.
    Pòlínà   gbà   Ńkítẹ́ — m   úkwú.
    | | | |

Lex. T. [PAULINA   KICKED   DOG   ME   FOOT.]
Lit. T. [[Paulina   kicked   my   dog a foot.]]

Fr. T.   (Paulina   kicked   my   dog.)

18. Pòlínà   shù   Ńkítẹ́m   ọ́kwụ́

    Pòlínà   shù   Ńkítẹ́ — m   ọ́kwụ́

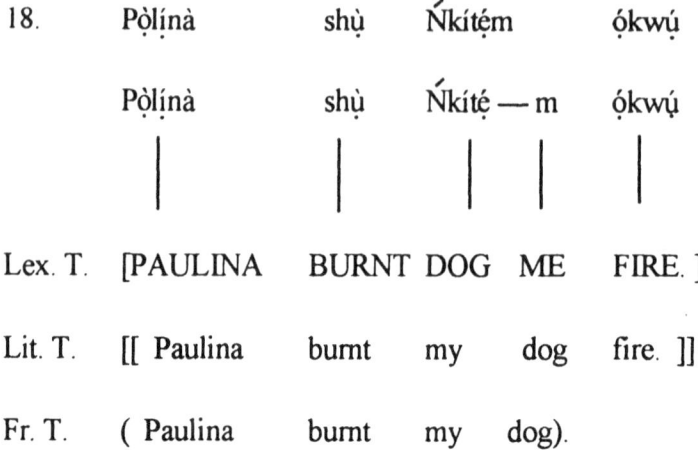

Lex. T. [PAULINA   BURNT DOG   ME   FIRE.]

Lit. T. [[Paulina   burnt   my   dog   fire.]]

Fr. T.   (Paulina   burnt   my   dog).

According to the reasoning of those grammarians who would not respect the Igbo SL community's world picture,[12] "It does not make sense" to accept that the Igbo people "really think" that one **stings** a needle as suggested by the lexical translation of sentence example 14 above; for, according to the same kind of reasoning being discussed here, "everyone knows" that you may use needles to 'sting' (i.e that you may 'sting' with needles) in a manner of speaking, but that you most certainly do **not** sting the needles themselves! Therefore, grammarians of Igbo language who endorse the position just outlined would characteristically **not** provide any English TL literal level of translation for the Igbo

---

12. See, for example, P.A. NWACHUKWU's (1985) study of so-called "inherent complement verbs in Igbo". The constructs in quote marks in my discussion above are **not** quotations of NWACHUKWU'S (1985) own statements, but do reflect his position and that of many other grammarians I accuse here of not respecting SL world picture.

SL in question, and would analyse the Igbo construct gbà Ntútú [[stung a needle]] simply as **one** principal lexical item, translatable freely to English as 'injected' and comprising the two supposedly mutually dependent auxiliary constituent language units gbà (stung) and Ntútú (needle).[13] Thus, such a grammarian would, **following in fact the English TL thought** in the matter (instead of the thought of the corresponding translated Igbo SL), analyse the Igbo sentence example 14, re-presented below, as containing only one grammatical object, Ọgọ́chúkwú, while Ntụ́tụ́ (needle) is then, as explained already, **not** seen as an object at all but merely as an **auxiliary** lexical item **completing** the communication function of gbà (stung) such that both units supposedly express the same information as that of the English 'injected'. To make my illustration of the position of the targeted grammarian easier to appreciate, I translate below the sentence example 14 in question using the translation convention characteristic of such grammarians.

14. Ńgbōàfò   gbà   Ọgọ́chúkwú   Ǹtụ́tụ́.

     NAME OF   stung   NAME OF   needle
     PERSON   PERSON

     Ngboafo   injected   Ogochukwu.

---

13. Note the non-specification with the English free transaction of what in the Igbo sentence example 14 is apparently the instrument - i.e Ntụ́tụ́ (needle) - of the 'stinging'. For the particular communication I have in mind, Ǹtútú (needle) of the Igbo sentence example 14 is in fact **not** presented by the Igbo as an instrument. The same reasoning applies to the other pertinent Igbo sentence examples. I listed above for this discussion: Thus, àgbàdà (dagger) of the Igbo sentence example 13 above is also **not** presented in the Igbo as an instrument; etc.

By the same reasoning as for sentence example 14, and using the same type of translating convention, mà àgbàdà [[pierced a dagger]] of sentence example 13 is interpreted as 'stabbed' and there is only one object in the sentence, Àdáéké; mù Ńbọ́ [[pinched nails]] of sentence example 15 is interpreted as 'pinched' and there is only one object in the sentence, Pọ̀línà; gbà égbè [[shot a gun]] of sentence example 16 is interpreted as 'shot' and there is only one object in the sentence, éwúm (my goat); gbà ụ́kwụ́ [kicked a foot]] of sentence example 17 is interpreted as 'kicked' and there is only one object in the sentence, Ńkítẹ́m (my dog); shụ̀ ọ́kwụ́ [[burnt fire]] of sentence example 18 is interpreted as 'burnt' and there is only one object in the sentence, Ńkítẹ́m (my dog).

13. Ụ́nọ̀kà   mà   Àdáéké   àgbàdà.

    NAME OF   pierced   NAME OF   dagger
    PERSON   PERSON

    Unoka   stabbed   Adaeke.

15. Ngbōàfọ̀   mù   Pọ̀línà   Ńbọ́

    NAME OF   pinched   NAME OF   nail
    PERSON   PERSON

    Ngboafo   pinched   Paulina.

72

16. | Ụ́nọ̀kà | gbà | éwúḿ | égbè.
    | NAME OF PERSON | shot | goat me | gun

    Unoka shot my goat.

17. | Pòlínà | gbà | Ńkítẹ́ḿ | ụ́kwụ́.
    | NAME OF PERSON | kicked | dog me | foot

    Paulina kicked my dog.

18. | Pòlínà | shụ̀ | Ńkítẹ́m | ọ́kwụ́.
    | NAME OF PERSON | burnt | dog me | fire.

    Paulina burnt my dog.

Now, my point here is that the position outlined in the last paragraph above is the grammarian's unwillingness or inability to accept the facts of the SL community's world picture as they are, as well as a case of too much respect by the grammarian for how

TL tradition expects all languages to work. Contrary to the said position of 'making sense', I stress here that **the function of a literal translation is precisely to expose with TL any oddity of SL community's world picture** noticed from the TL community's point of view, NOT to destroy the very basis of a literal translation needed for the grammatical description of the SL by eliminating or hiding or camouflaging such oddity[14] in the name of 'making sense'. Once this position is sincerely adopted, it becomes possible to begin to understand the apparent strange logic of a particular language community's world picture.

Consider for illustration the Igbo sentence examples 13 to 18 again, with only English literal translations provided this time for convenience.

13. Ụnọkà   mà   Àdáéké   àgbàdà.

    [[Unoka   pierced   Adaeke   a dagger.]]

---

14. Although languages may differ in unpredictable ways from one another, they are also often surprisingly similar to one another. So, it is to be expected that for several source texts (STs) and corresponding equivalent target texts (TTs) of two given languages considered, one may discover no significant differences of world picture. Because the function of a literal translation is in fact to expose with TL any **oddity** (from the TL community's point of view) of SL community's world picture, it is pointless to insist on presenting TT literal translations of such STs where SL community's and TL community's world pictures coincidentally do appear to be identical.

14. Ńgbōàfọ̀   gbà   Ọ̀gọ́chúkwú   Ntụ́tụ́.
    [[Ngboafo stung   Ogochukwu   a needle.]]

15. Ńgbōàfọ̀   mù   Pọ̀lị́nà   Ńbọ́.
    [[Ngboafo pinched Paulina   nails.]]

16. Ụ́nọ̀kà   gbà   éwúm   égbè.
    [[Unoka   shot   my goat   a gun.]]

17. Pọ̀lị́nà   gbà   Ńkítẹ́m   ụ́kwụ́.
    [[Paulina kicked   my   dog a foot.]]

18. Pọ̀lị́nà   shụ̀   Ńkítẹ́m   ọ́kwụ́.
    [[Paulina burnt   my dog   fire.]]

Surprisingly, we can explain the apparent strangeness of Igbo thought displayed with the literal translations above by referring to what obtains, albeit to a much smaller degree, in the **English** TL semantic structure. I take the following three English sentences in addition for the demonstration.

19. Robin Hood shot the arrow with characteristic superlative skill.

20. "Shoot the pig!", cried the terrorist.

21. James Bond shot the pistol at the same time as his assailant reached for the bomb.

The meaning of the word 'shoot' in sentences 19 and 21 on the one hand **differs** from that of 'shoot' in sentence 20 on the other hand. In sentence 20, it is **a person**, "the pig", that is condemned to suffer the effect of the shooting; in sentences 19 and 21 on the other hand, neither the **arrow** nor the **pistol** (which are indeed shot) suffers the effect of the shooting – rather, they are **caused to shoot**, respectively by Robin Hood and James Bond, such that some persons then presumably suffer the effect of the arrow and the gun being caused to shoot. Thus, **what** was shot[1] (i.e, caused to shoot) for sentences 19 and 21 was the arrow or the pistol, and **who** was shot[2] (i.e, suffered the effect of the arrow's or gun's shooting), in exactly the same sense as that of 'shoot' for sentence 20, was (presumably) some person.

Now, the Igbo thought for gbà égbè [[shot a gun]] of sentence example 16 above is akin to that of the English 'shot the arrow' and 'shot the pistol' of the English sentences 19 and 21 above respectively!

16. Únọkà   gbà   éwúm̀   égbè

    [[Unoka   shot   my goat   a gun]

19. Robin Hood shot the arrow with characteristic superlative skill.

21. James Bond shot the pistol at the same time as his assailant reached for the bomb.

And éwúm (my goat) then suffered the effect of that shooting of the Igbo sentence example 16.

Similarly, when, according to sentence example 13, the Igbo say that "Únọkà pierced Àdáéké a dagger", we should be understood to be stating that Únọkà caused the dagger to pierce, and that the person pierced was Àdáéké.

13. Únọkà   mà   Àdáéké   àgbàdà.

    [[Unoka   pierced   Adaeke   a   dagger .]]

    (Unoka   stabbed   Adaeke.)

77

In sentence example 14, by "Ńgbọ̀àfọ̀ stung Ògóchúkwú a needle", we should understand that the needle was caused to 'sting' and that Ògóchúkwú was 'stung'

14. Ńgbọ́àfọ̀   gbà   Ògóchúkwú   Ǹtụ̀tụ́.

    [[Ngboafo   stung   Ogochukwu   a needle.]]

    (Ngboafo   injected   Ogochukwu.)

In sentence example, 15, by Ngboafo pinched Paulina nails we should understand that Ngboafo's nails were caused to pinch, and that Paulina was pinched.

15. Ńgbọ́àfọ̀   mù   Pọ̀lịnà   Ńbọ́.

    [[Ngboafo   pinched   Paulina   nails.]]

    (Ngboafo   pinched   Paulina.)

In sentence example 17, by 'Paulina kicked my dog a foot' we should understand that Paulina's foot was caused to kick, and that my dog was kicked.

17. Pọ̀lịnà   gbà   Ńkítẹ́ḿ   ụ̀kwụ́.

    [[Paulina   kicked   my   dog   a foot.]]

    (Paulina   kicked   my   dog.)

Finally, in sentence example 18, by 'Paulina burnt my dog fire' we should understand that fire was caused to burn and that my dog was burnt.

18. Pòlínà   shù   Nkítẹ́m   ọ́kwụ́.

    [[Paulina   burnt   my dog   fire.]]

    (Paulina   burnt   my dog.)

So, to obtain with English sentence construct 20 above essentially the same type of thought as found in the Igbo sentences 13 to 18 and innumerable others, we could modify it to produce the strange sentence example 22 — as follows.

20. "Shoot the pig!", cried the terrorist.

22. * "Shoot the pig the gun!", cried the terrorist.

Following, then, the same reasoning I used to analyse sentences 13 to 18 above, we should understand by the strange English sentence example 22 above that the gun is to be caused to shoot, and that "the pig" is the individual to be shot. Thus, contrary to TL-based analyses of grammarians like NWACHUKWU (1985) who do **not** respect the SL world pictures, we see from our analysis of English sentence example 22 that each of the Igbo sentences 13 to 18 has in fact **two** (NOT one) direct grammatical objects as exemplified in sentence example 22 where we have

(i) What is to be shot (i.e , caused
                                to shoot),
                              the gun; and

(ii) Who is to be shot (i.e., suffer the effect of the shooting),
                                    "the pig".

    We may conclude from the foregoing illustrations and discussion that when SL community world picture is sincerely respected through satisfactory literal translations we can learn with TL quite a lot of formerly unsuspected facts about the SL community's grammar. On the contrary, whenever the grammarian distorts SL community's world picture through, for example, too much concern with "making sense" (according to the rules of making sense as usually understood in the TL community) then the claims made about the SL grammar are to that extent impoverished and invalid.

CHAPTER **4**

SYNTAX AND GRAMMAR

In Generative Grammar, Syntax = Grammar

In Generative Grammar, right from its official beginnings in 1957, we have been lectured again and again about a new, revolutionary, conception of Grammar as "any mechanism/device of some sort" for "generating" (i.e, for **constructing**) all (and only) the well-formed sentences of any given language.[1]

---

1 Cf. CHOMSKY, N. (1962: 52)

> The grammar, then, is a device that (in particular) specifies the infinite set of well-formed sentences and assigns to each of these one or more structural descriptions.

81

The mechanism/device, it is usually further explained, is in fact "a system of rules" (i.e, a system of **procedures**).[2] Since 1965 especially, the 'system of rules' has been arranged in three major sets, viz:

(i) the syntactic or syntax set;

(ii) the semantic or meaning set; and

(iii) the phonological or sound set.

Of these, rather confusingly, only the syntactic or syntax rules have been recognised to be "generative" (i.e., constructional)[3] in virtually all **mainstream** didactic pronouncements about Grammar in Generative Grammar, the semantic or meaning rules and the phonological or sound rules being merely

---

2 Cf. CHOMSKY, N. (1962: 52)
　　On the basis of a limited experience
　　with the data of speech, each normal
　　human has developed for himself a thorough
　　competence in his native language. This
　　competence can be represented, to an as
　　yet undetermined extent, as a system of rules
　　that we can call the **grammar** of his language

3. Cf. CHOMSKY, N. (1965: 15-16,) for instance.

"interpretive" (i.e., comprehensional)[4] – which simply amounts to saying really that the syntax or syntactic rules are those for generating or constructing the sentences of the language, while the meaning or semantic rules and the sound or phonological rules are for comprehending the meanings and pronunciations respectively of the constructed sentences. In other words, the "system of rules" for "generating the sentences of any language" which Grammar is identified to be[5] is in fact a syntax/syntactic system of rules; that is, Syntax = Grammar![6]

Now, intellectual paradigms are free, even encouraged, to introduce new terms and usages into scholarship in order to distance themselves on specific issues from past ignorance, and thus highlight their own new or novel, peculiar insights regarding

---

4. Cf. CHOMSKY, N. (1965: 16):
    Both the phonological and semantic components are
    therefore purely interpretive.

5. See the quotation of footnote 2 above where "grammar" is defined as a "system of rules". See also footnote 1.

6. Thus, Generative Grammar actually uses, simultaneously, the following two different interpretations of the term "Grammar" as "system of rules":
    a. a broad interpretation, whereby Grammar = Syntax, Semantics, and Phonology;
    b. a narrow interpretation, whereby Grammar = Syntax.

    In the former (where Grammar = Syntax, Semantics, and Phonology), Grammar is understood as 'the study of sentences construction or generation' (i.e., Syntax) plus 'the study of sentences comprehension or interpretation,' (i.e., Semantics and Phonology). In the latter interpretation (where Grammar = Syntax), "Grammar" is synonymous with generation/ construction.

the phenomena studied. Unfortunately, however, Generative Grammar's novel usage of the term 'syntax' as synonymous with 'Grammar' and interpretable as the 'system of rules' for sentences generation undermines Linguistic Theory critically in the following two main ways. First, given that, as we saw in Chapter Two of this book, Grammar = Linguistics in Generative Grammar, it becomes clear that since (as we have just seen) Syntax = Grammar in Generative Grammar, then Syntax = Linguistics in Generative Grammar! Which is again in fact why Generativism has been characterised in this book as a **syntacticist** approach to the study of Language. I have already discussed at some length the intellectual paucity of the linguistic theory which derives from this syntacticist perspective of Language; so, no further comment is needed here to expose the lamentable methodological credentials of the scientific paradigm concerned. Second, deliberately or unwittingly, the confusing usage of 'syntax' in Generative Grammar obfuscates, and even erodes, the standard modern Linguistics conception of 'syntax' which nobody has yet seriously contested – thus vitiating the conduct of linguistic investigation in that domain and emasculating the worth of its resulting Linguistic Theory. In the rest of this chapter, I opt therefore categorically for the abandonment of Generative Grammar's usage of 'syntax' **which lacks any content whatsoever not already attributable to 'Grammar'**[7] and situate **within** Grammar the revised modern standard conception of 'syntax' adopted in Performative Linguistics.

---

7   Even if in Generative Grammar one opted to use 'syntax' exclusively for 'the study of sentences construction' and 'Grammar' exclusively for the study of sentences construction **plus** the semantic and phonological

The domain of Syntax

In line with the standard modern usage, I define 'Syntax' as 'the study of the **external** structuring of words' – in contradistinction with 'Morphology', which is 'the study of the **internal** structuring of words'. Traditionally, the lower limit of the subject matter of Syntax is the **phrase** meaningful form unit, and its upper limit the **sentence** form meaningful unit; but, following current Linguistics insights whereby it is nowadays fairly widely acknowledged that there are structured units of Language higher than the sentence, I understand Syntax to cover the study of all supra-word-level symbolisation structures. Accordingly, Syntax is both a part of Symbolics in Linguistics (because it studies a symbolisation level of Language), and a part of Grammar (because it is a structural study of Language) in Linguistics.

Symbolics and Grammar

To appreciate the exact position of Syntax within both Symbolics and Grammar, it is useful here to first determine the relationship between Symbolics and Grammar. Next, we shall also establish the constituency of Symbolics as follows:

---

comprehension of those sentences, we would still be left with the stark incongruity that **there is nothing in the semantic and phonological comprehension of sentences which is not already in their semantic and phonological construction** in 'Syntax' – thus rendering 'syntax' again essentially **equal to** "Grammar" in Generative Grammar.

We recall that Language is made up of **both** thought (or 'meaning') **and** symbolisation (or 'form') **only**, and that Linguistics, the scientific study of the phenomenon Language, is made up of two and only two immediate constituents with respect to Language content – viz, (i) Semantics, the scientific study of Language thought or meaning; and (ii) Symbolics, the scientific study of Language symbolisation or form.

LINGUISTICS (the scientific study of Language)

SYMBOLICS, the scientific study of symbolisation/'form'
SEMANTICS, the scientific study of thought/ 'meaning'

Fig. 5: *Linguistics = Semantics + Symbolics*

We recall also that Grammar is no more and no less than Structural (or Textual) Semantics plus Structural (or Textual) Symbolics.

GRAMMAR (the study of Language structure)

Structural or Textual Symbolics
Structural or Textual Semantics

Fig. 10: Grammar = Textual Semantics + Textual Symbolics

We recall further that considering Language in terms of both its structure and use, Linguistics as a whole comprises Structural or Textual Semantics plus Use or Contextual Semantics on the one hand, and Structural or Textual Symbolics plus Use or Contextual Symbolics on the other hand:

LINGUISTICS (the scientific study of Languages.)

Symbolics	Structural or Textual Symbolics	Use or Contextual Symbolics
Semantics	Structural or Textual Semantics	Use or Contextual Semantics
	Grammar	Pragmatics

Fig. 12: Linguistics = *Textual Semantics and Contextual Semantics.*
+
Textual Symbolics and Contextual Symbolics

From the above, we see then that (like Semantics, the other major constituent of Linguistics) **only part of Symbolics is part of Grammar** (i.e., the textual or structural component) – the contextual or use Symbolics being indeed part of Linguistics as a whole, but definitely **not** part of Grammar. Syntax, as the study of a symbolisation level of Language, is therefore part of the **Structural Symbolics** part of Grammar; and, given the foregoing, **it does NOT begin to make sense to posit semantic inputs within the syntactic processes component of Language** – as in mainstream Generative Grammar.

Speech and Symbolics

To situate Syntax precisely within the Structural Symbolics component of Grammar where it belongs, we need to determine in some detail the constituency of Symbolics in Linguistics. Unlike Generative Grammar's premise whereby Language symbolisation is essentially **phonological** (i.e, phonic) and the study of Language symbolisation is necessarily a study of speech,[8] a cardinal tenet of Performative Linguistics is that there are **several** kinds of Language symbolisation – whereby there are, correspondingly, several kinds of Symbolics, the study of Language symbolisation. Performative Grammar thus rejects the so-called Primacy of Speech Principle of modern Linguistics[9] for the structural study of Language whereby Language supposedly is somehow fundamentally spoken.

Towards dethroning the Primacy of Speech Principle

Given the above assumption, modern linguistic studies have to date categorically emphasised the investigation of the spoken variety. The excessive emphasis is reflected, for example, in

---

8. See, for example, Generative Grammar's innumerable exclusive references to **speakers** and **hearers** in discussing Language (symbolisation) - as, say, in (CHOMSKY (1965: 4):

    A grammar of a language purports to be a description of the ideal speaker-hearer's intrinsic competence.

9. In line with "the recent flood of publications trying to come to terms with one of the more conspicuous paradoxes of modern linguistics" (COULMAS, 1990 : 173).

such anthropocentric statements about the nature of Language as that Language is a "uniquely human activity",[10] that Language is "a system of human communication of speech sounds used as arbitrary symbols"[11] or that "speech, many authorities believe, is what makes humans human..."[12] The primary motivation for this overwhelming emphasis is, of course, to show that humans are a unique class of beings, since **they** have speech and 'lower' animals do **not**[13].

The overwhelming majority of Linguists, when directly consulted about the matter, would readily admit that sound is only a **medium** for Language, and that Language is **not** speech. Many twentieth-century studies which show non-humans[14] communicating fluently with humans via **non**-speech communication media tend to support the just-mentioned 'official' position of Linguistics — throwing into confusion, therefore, the traditional lore that Language is essentially speech,

---

10. PEARSON, B. L. (1977 : 3)

11. PEARSON, B.L. (1977:372)

12. TIME-LIFE (1973:99)

13 Cf. RUMBAUGH (1977:56) :

> The fact that 'language' has always implied '**human** language' had led to a confusion of two terms, 'speech' and 'language', which although certainly related, are not at all the same... Many linguists thus came to consider 'speech' and 'language' as quasi-synonyms, and consequently felt justified in studying language by investigating the acoustic, physical manifestation of speech.

14. For example LINDEN (1976), RUMBAUGH (1977), and TERRACE (1979)

and raising the fundamental question as to what exactly is meant by 'Language' for that lore.

Unfortunately, the emphasis of modern Linguistics on the study of the **spoken** variety of Language is not just a matter of preference; it presupposes that in some not always clearly stated sense, speech is actually much more important than any other medium for Language. Thus, the so-called Primacy of Speech remains enshrined in current Linguistics texts and is still taught as objective truth within introductory courses for Linguistics[15]. It is this special brand of modern linguistic studies excessive pre-occupation with the scientific investigation of speech that is **rejected** in Performative Linguistics, as shown hereafter.

Speech and writing

The original motivation of modern Linguistics for declaring the so-called cardinal principle that "spoken language is more basic than written language" was to redress the intellectually disturbing imbalance between the study of speech and that of writing, which imbalance was created in Greek antiquity to favour writing and maintained doggedly for centuries in Traditional Grammar. In Greek antiquity, for instance, the descriptive framework for Phonetics was the Greek alphabet,

---

15. For example, LYONS, J. (1981:11) says:

> It is one of the cardinal principles of modern linguistics that spoken language is more basic than written language

and statements took the form of accounts of the pronunciation of the letters of it.[16] The Stoics of Greek antiquity, in particular,[17] distinguished three aspects of a written letter, viz:

> its phonetic value ...,[18] its written shape...,[19] and the name[20] by which it was designated... These three properties of letters continued to be distinguished throughout antiquity, their Latin names being potestas (power), figura (shape), and nomen (name).

But, in supposedly correcting the said imbalance of ancient linguistic studies, modern Linguistics has inadvertently succeeded in creating another imbalance – in favour of **speech** this time – which imbalance will be shown, hereafter, to be completely unjustified.

The first and most widely used reason to support the primacy of speech is that of **historical priority**.[21] By this it is claimed that speech antedates writing: in historical time writing is a relatively recent phenomenon in human societies, having been invented in

---

16. ROBINS, R.H. (1979:23)

17. According to ROBINS, R.H. (1979 : 24)

18. E.g., [b]

19. E.g. , B.

20. E.g. , the name 'bee' for the letter B.

21. For this and other proposed types of priority described and discussed in this section see LYONS, J. (1981 : 12 - 16)

Sumer in ancient Mesopotamia[22] about 3,100 B.C.; and there have been many human communities without any writing systems; but human societies, for as long as they have existed, are understood to have used spoken language. The claim itself of historical priority as stated above is **not** disputable; but it does **not** prove that speech is more basic than writing, if by "more basic" we are to understand not just "older" (which is the basis of the argument and **not** the argument itself) but also *ipso facto* inherently more important (and therefore deserving of much more scientific attention), because "more recent" does **not necessarily** amount to "less important" by that very fact. For illustration, the gestures of so-called "sign language" are arguably **much older** than speech as communicative vehicles in human societies; but advancing conclusive evidence for or against that thesis is not even a burning subject for modern Linguistics; and, as such, Linguists will not be particularly impressed and pay more attention to the gestural language variety than to the spoken, merely because it has become obvious that the former (i.e; gestural language) antedates the latter (i.e., spoken language) in historical time.

The **structural priority** argument claims that writing is a reflection or copy of speech – such that the structure of writing is based on that of speech, to which it supposedly corresponds. This thesis is **patently false** when applied to the so-called "semic" or meaning scripts – of which pictographies (whose pictures represent thought **directly**) and ideographies (whose conventional characters represent thought **directly**) are exemplars

---

22. In the land area within which present-day Iran and Iraq are located.

— where writing represents thought **directly,** instead of (via) speech. But even in the so-called "phonetic" scripts where writing does represent speech directly – of which syllabaries (in which writing symbols represent syllables) and alphabets (in which individual written letters stand for phonemes of specific languages) are examples – the correspondence between speech and writing tends to be progressively more loose with time, reflecting more and more two distinct kinds of evolution of two symbolisation types, instead of a domination of writing structure by speech structure as implied by the structural priority argument. Take, for illustration, the words **knight** and **night**: first of all, the letters **k, g** and **h** in these words have **no** individual speech unit equivalents which they are supposed to represent if writing is truly just for representing speech; secondly, the letter **k** there distinguishes the word **knight** from **night** (and is hence distinctive in writing as phonemes are distinctive in speech), while speech makes no overt formal distinction between the two words in modern English – showing once more that speech and writing tend to incarnate communicative rules peculiar to their respective natures.

Thirdly, the **functional priority** argument states[23] that even in the most literate societies of today the spoken variety of Language:

> is used for a wider range of purposes than the written, and writing serves as a functional substitute for speech only in situations which make vocal-auditory communication impossible, unreliable or inefficient. And the invention of the telephone and

---

23. According to LYONS, J. (1981 : 14)

tape-recorder has made possible the use of the spoken language in circumstances in which written language would have been employed. It was for the purposes of reliable communication at a distance and the preservation of important legal, religious and commercial documents that writing was originally invented.

As is quite obvious from the above quotation, writing was invented precisely for those very situations where it is functionally relevant as a communication mode, just as there are situations where speech or gestures are preferable or even indispensable. Thus, the functional priority argument really states no more and no less than the truism that speech and writing are useful communication modes for different communication situations consonant with their respective natures. To show the functional superiority of speech over writing, then, it is **not** enough merely to list a higher number of uses for speech than for writing, were that convincingly feasible, but to demonstrate conclusively that speech is somehow **inherently** (NOT accidentally) more functional than writing. Nobody has yet done this, apparently; on the contrary, all the available evidence points to the fact that societies become more literate (that is, write more and read more writings) as they become more and more developed; and therefore that writing has become more and more (instead of less) functional in modern societies which, being increasingly developed, have many more communication needs than the relatively much simpler societies of the distant past.

Finally, the **biological priority** argument, which states that "human beings are genetically programmed, not only to acquire language, but also... to produce and recognise speech-sounds"[24] is perhaps the most trivial of the arguments for the primacy of speech vis-à-vis any other medium of Language. If we have been "genetically programmed" to acquire speech sounds, then we are equally "genetically programmed" to produce and recognise writing marks, because they too **are** Language elements and we have been genetically programmed to acquire Language; for nobody, to my knowledge, has yet demonstrated otherwise – i.e.; that we are supposedly genetically programmed for spoken Language but not for written Language. The biological priority argument could perhaps begin to aspire to some merit if it hinged on the assertion that the sound recognition organs (i.e, the ears) are biologically much more basic in the evolutionary scheme than the writing recognition organs (i.e, the eyes). But such a line of argument, were it not already false, would not be tenable either: for the so-called ''speech organs'', as every competent Linguist knows, were **not** originally designed by nature for speech as such, any more than ''writing organs'' for writing, but were conventionally adapted in relatively recent biological time to the cultural ends of communication; so, any genetic programming under the circumstances must be of some very general potential for Language (communication), rather than of the specific particularities of either speech or writing, say.

From the above discussion, we have seen not only that the four standard arguments for defending the so-called cardinal principle in modern Linguistics that "speech is more basic than writing" are invalid but also that they even provide **wrong**

---

24. LYONS, J. (1981 : 14)

criteria for justifying the principle. What is needed to justify the principle is to demonstrate conclusively that speech is inherently 'more linguistic' (whatever that amounts to in reality) than any other Language medium. Once the above is understood, then the absurdity of the primacy of speech principle should become fairly obvious: in short, **all symbolisation systems are equal**.

The character of symbolisation

As we saw in Chapter One of this book, symbolisation is linguistic by virtue of the fact that it represents thought for communication; therefore, any type of Language symbolisation is one particular manifestation or realisation of the symbolisation component of Language – such that, as we also saw in this chapter, even where writing is said to represent speech directly (in so-called phonetic scripts like the alphabetic writing system being used here), it symbolises thought ultimately for communication, according to rules intrinsic to its own nature as marks rather than according to the nature of sound. The question does not begin to make sense, therefore, to ask which symbolisation type is ''more basic'' (i.e., ''more linguistic'' in nature?) than the other, since the phenomena being referred to are intrinsically different from one another in their respective individualities, are consequently linguistic (and thus communicative) in **inherently different ways** and as such are necessarily incomparable. It does make a lot of sense, however, to characterise symbolisation generally and then specify the peculiar nature of each particular manifestation of this (i.e; the symbolic) component of Language.

Language forms – that is, Language symbolisation types – are aspects of Language which are directly perceivable with the senses. Since we have **five** basic senses in all admittedly, it is correct to say that we also have in principle five types of symbolisation, viz:

(i) gustatory (taste) symbolisation;

(ii) olfactory (smell) symbolisation;

(iii) tactile (touch) symbolisation;

(iv) aural (hearing) symbolisation; and

(v) visual (sight) symbolisation.

Of these, we generally use the two last types (aural and visual) above – as in writing, gestures, and speech; exceptionally, as in Braille writing used by the visually handicapped, we sometimes also use the tactile type of symbolisation in linguistic communication. I shall therefore henceforth in this chapter assume that Symbolics, the science of Language symbolisation, should be seriously concerned with at least for now elucidating the specific natures of the gestural, speech, and graphic Language symbolisation types.

While Symbolics is the science of Language form in general, I shall henceforth call **Cherics**[25] the subscience of Symbolics concerned generally with studying the symbolisation of Language thought by **gestures** or "signs" in popular expression; **Graphics** is the subscience of Symbolics concerned generally with the study of the symbolisation of Language thought by writing; and **Phonics** is the subscience of Symbolics generally concerned with the study of the symbolisation of Language thought by sound. The three next immediate layers of Symbolics are Text Symbolics, Sentence Symbolics, and Phrase Symbolics – concerned with the scientific study of Language symbolisation at suprasentential, sentential, and phrasal Language units levels respectively. Next, there is **Semics**, the study of concepts-**representing** forms, called "semes" in Performative Linguistics, **Emics**, the study of sub-semic semantically distinctive minimal form units which may be called "emes", **Etics** the study of the physical qualities of minimal form units, and **Nuclear Symbolics**, the study of the ultimate material constituents of minimal form units – according to Performative Linguistics. The above layers of Symbolics may be presented diagrammatically as follows:

---

25. I have coined this and other derived terms concerning gestural Language from "cheremes" "the manual equivalent of spoken phonemes" according to TERRACE, H.S. (1979: 363)

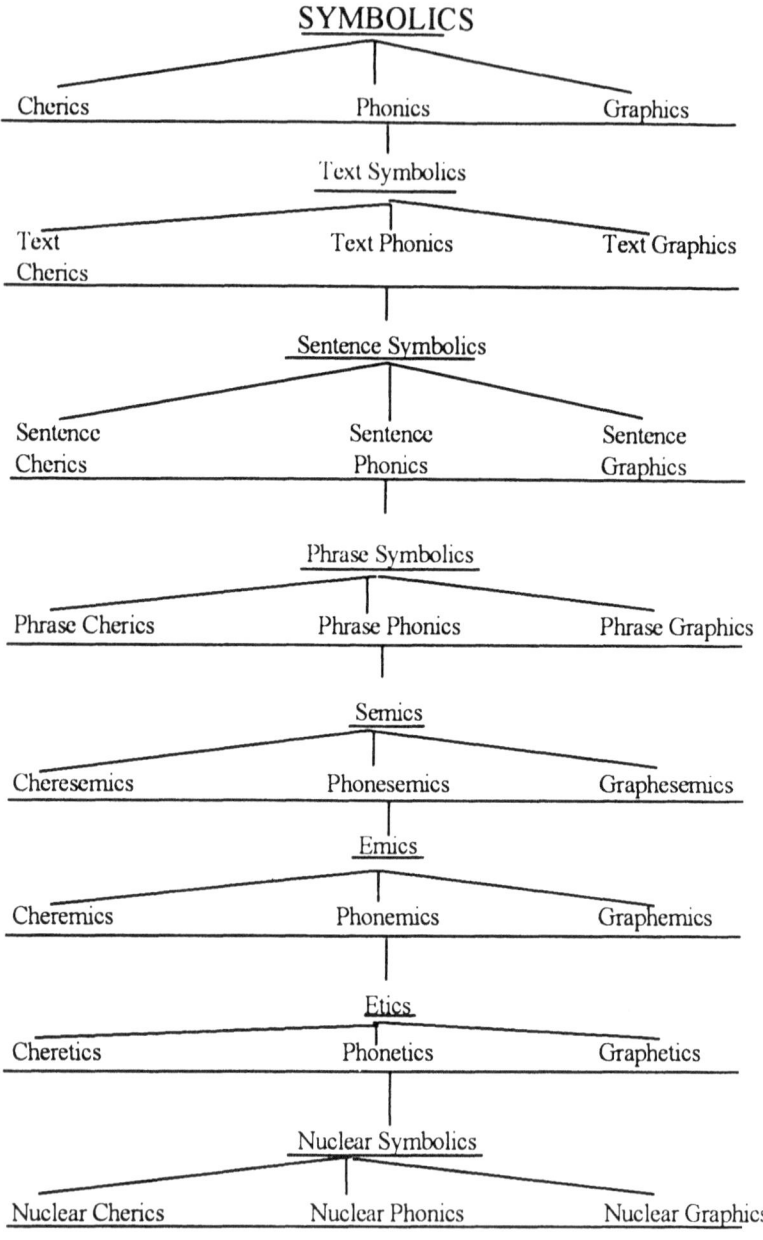

Fig. 14: The Constituency of Symbolics

As implied in the above discussion, any of the above-named layers of Symbolics may be studied structurally or non-structurally, or both structurally and non-structurally. For an illustration of what could be involved, and how rich Linguistics science could become with a proper study of other symbolisation types besides sound, let me present below possible principles of Graphetics and Nuclear Graphics subsciences in Symbolic Linguistics (or Symbolics).

Elements of Graphetics

Following SWEET, H. (1902 : 1), Phonetics has been defined as "the science of speech sounds". I would define Phonetics as "the science of the physical qualities of minimal sound units of Language". Accordingly, Graphetics is for me "the science of the physical qualities of minimal writing units of Language".

According to HEFFNER (1952:3), two broad types of investigation are subsumed in Phonetics – viz:

(i) **genetic** investigation, covering the study of the movements of the speech organs which produce the sound units; and

(ii) **gennemic** investigation, covering the study of the sound units as acoustic phenomena after they have been produced.

BLOOMFIELD (1933 : 75) presents the two broad divisions in Phonetics in more familiar language respectively as **physiological** and **acoustic** Phonetics. For PIKE, (1943 : 14), the two branches are **articulatory** and **acoustic** Phonetics. Phoneticians are generally agreed with respect to the two main divisions of Phonetics presented above that **instrumental** Phonetics is **not really** a third, separate branch of Phonetics as such, but is subsumed in **both** articulatory (or physiological or genetic) Phonetics on the one hand **and** acoustic (or gennemic) Phonetics on the other hand. Thus, we can similarly divide Graphetics into the two broad branches – viz:

(i) **genetic** or **fabricatory** Graphetics, concerning the investigation of the movements of the writing organs which produce the marks, and

(ii) **gennemic** or **visual** Graphetics, concerning the marks themselves as physical phenomena, after they have been produced.

Experimental or instrumental Graphetics should then be subsumed in both branches of Graphetics.

The essential unit in Phonetics is called a **phone**; that of Graphetics should be called a **graph**; and a **phoneme** is a meaning-distinctive phone in a given language studied by **Phonemics**, while a **grapheme** is correspondingly a meaning-distinctive graph in a particular language, studied by **Graphemics.** Just as phones can be studied for their characteristic sound-wave features in Phonetics, so graphs should be investigated for their peculiar physical properties as visual material in Graphetics.

Nuclear Graphics

For me, a major discovery in Graphics is that each graph is actually made up of a number or combination of **minimal**

writing strokes, which I call **graphic particles**, or **graphicles** for short. For example, the letter C is made up of only one curve graphicle C; the capital letter B is made up of **two** graphicles – i.e, a vertical stroke. I, and the curved stroke ⊃ joined twice to the two halves of the vertical stroke. This discovery of the graphicle is of crucial importance for the teaching of basic writing (to children and grown-ups who have never learned to write), for it helps to arrange the characters or writing units of a writing system according to the inherent order of complexity or difficulty of their component graphicles. The discovery has already been applied to good effect in the book *Teach Your Child to Write* (UWAJEH, M.K.C. 1993).

The notion of the graphicle can be also used to analyse satisfactorily any writing characters, for a functional evaluation of any system of writing. For example, it has been shown in UWAJEH (1993) already mentioned above that all the capital letters of the Latin-derived so-called English alphabet are actually created from only **six** basic graphicles – listed as follows:

(i)   /
(ii) \
(iii) —
(iv) |
(v)   ⊃
(vi) ⊂

Also ABDULLAHI's (1992) *Tafi Alphabet* can by graphicles analysis be shown to be one of the simplest writing systems known so far. Its basic building blocks of characters, called "digits" by ABDULLAHI, are six in number, three of which are presented below for illustration:

Using graphicles analysis, it is obvious that this system of writing employs only two graphicles, 1 and -, for its six "digits" or characters.

Equality of all Language forms

Modern Linguistics has to date, I repeat, generally paid too much attention to the phonic or sound aspect of symbolisation – sometimes to the point of almost systematically equating speech to Language, often to the point of almost completely ignoring the study of other types of symbolisation – as even a cursory look at textbooks of modern Linguistics readily confirms. Although very much neglected even up to current times in Linguistics, other types of symbolisation besides sound are highly complex in their different ways, and equally interesting or even fascinating for the Linguist.

The position adopted here is that one type of symbolisation is neither better nor worse intrinsically than another for representing thought or 'meaning'. The Big Mistake, as I see it, is to judge one type of symbolisation system–structure with the yardstick devised specifically to highlight the attractive particularities of another type of symbolisation – very much as Linguists have also for centuries now erroneously attempted to establish the supposed non-linguistic status of non-human animal means of communication by appealing to their lack of the specific characteristics found in **human** languages.[26]

Sound does **not**, therefore, take precedence over other symbolisation types – either in terms of seniority (gestures may well have been around for much longer and been used more universally by humans before sounds), or in terms of utility (deaf and dumb people cope marvellously well, thank you, with gestural language, and it is at least plausible that other people besides monks and nuns would be as efficient in that expression mode as they are with speech if by cultural accident they had not been limited to using the speech medium much more matter-of-factedly), or in terms of independence (no type of symbolisation is completely self-sufficient in the representation of thought for communication; each mode tends to borrow from and depend on some other mode). For the above and other similar reasons, it is recognised in Performative Linguistics that each type of symbolisation manifests certain strengths **and** certain weaknesses as well (depending on the particular factors being considered), which derive from that symbolisation type's specific nature – such that, in the final analysis, **all symbolisation types**

---

26. See UWAJEH, M.K.C. (1990 : 116)
That "Language equals human language" is an old refrain without any intellectual depth... It may be quite comforting for our human ego, but poor science and poorer philosophy, to set about defining language such that only human communication systems qualify as language, and then swoon with wonder that animal communication systems do not have the very features we anthropocentrically attribute to language. We should expect animal communication systems to differ significantly from human communication systems (the opposite would be absurd, for animals are decidedly **not** humans !) in their individuality; but whether the former are language or not can only be decided through proper scholarship, not by dogmatic fiat...

are equal in their essence as representers (**directly or indirectly**) of thought, for communication.

Syntax and Structural Symbolics

Given the above fairly detailed picture of the character and constituency of Symbolics, it is now time to locate Syntax precisely within the Structural Symbolics component of Grammar: Syntax is the structural study of Language symbolisation at the post–semic levels – at the Phrase Symbolics, Sentence Symbolics, and Text Symbolics levels, that is. There are thus three layers of Syntax:

(i) Phrase Syntax, concerned with the structural study of phrase symbolisation;

(ii) Sentence Syntax, concerned with the structural study of sentence symbolisation; and

(iii) Text Syntax, concerned with the structural study of supra-sentential symbolisation.

At the sub-Syntax level of Structural Symbolics, the structural study of Language symbolisation at the Semic level of Symbolics is called **Morphology** – concerned with the study of word structure. Lower still, at the emic level, are **Emiology**, concerned with the structural study of the minimal semantically distinctive Language form units, and **Particle Symbolics**, concerned with identifying the ultimate constituents of Language symbolisation. Below is a diagrammatic presentation of the constituency of Structural Symbolics, within which the place of Syntax should be quite clear:

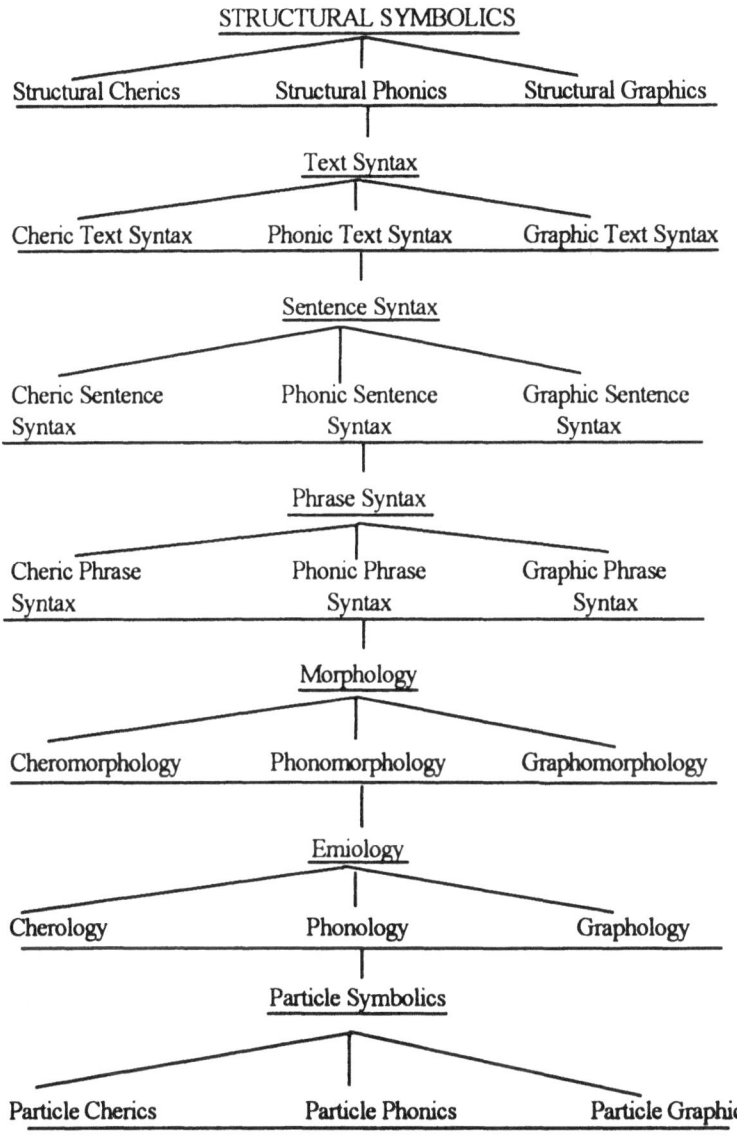

Fig. 15: The Constituency of Structural Symbolics

CHAPTER **5**

THE LEXICON AND GRAMMAR

The Traditional Grammar foundation of Generative Grammar

The lexicon is "the base" of Grammar, according to CHOMSKY (1965). In other words, for Generative Grammar since 1965, the lexicon of any given language constitutes the set of initial or foundation elements needed for constructing the sentences of that given language. This makes perfect sense, for there is hardly any Grammarian in modern Linguistics who would not readily admit that the lexical items of each given language (which make up its lexicon), are indeed the 'building blocks' as it were with which the sentences of that language are constructed. However, the characterisation of the constituents of the lexicon – i.e., the characterisation of any language's lexical items as such – in Generative Grammar does constitute a theoretically disastrous problem for the intellectual paradigm; and that is the issue I now proceed to address in this chapter.

The trouble with Generative Grammar's characterisation of lexical elements is that it is based on Traditional Grammar's so-called 'parts of speech'. This is **not** to say that Generative Grammar explicitly endorses all the tenets of Traditional Grammar's lore about parts of speech: for example, in line with the cardinal tenets of modern Linguistics, Generative Grammar purportedly **rejects** Traditional Grammar's definitions of those parts of speech in such terms as that "the verb is a doing word" or that "the noun is the name of any person, place, or thing". But by adopting Traditional Grammar's lexical categories (i.e., parts of speech) of "noun", "verb", "adjective", "article", etc. as the obligatory primitive elements for generating the sentences of languages (i.e., as the critical **base** for Grammar), Generative Grammar unwittingly endorses by implication Traditional Grammar's **classificatory scheme** for characterising lexical items, and is therefore also liable for Traditional Grammar's theoretic errors by which those lexical categories or parts of speech were formulated. More precisely speaking, when Generative Grammarians adopt wholesale Traditional Grammar's parts of speech of "noun", "verb", "adjective", "article", (also called "determiner"), "adverb", "preposition", "pronoun" and "conjunction" as the categories of lexical elements for constructing sentences in Grammar, they thereby **endorse** Traditional Grammar's parts of speech as a **correct** classificatory scheme to account for the lexical items of the lexicon-base of Grammar (for if the parts-of-speech classification scheme were not endorsed as such what else would be the point of using them for the base of any serious Grammar?); furthermore, by endorsing Traditional Grammar's parts of speech as a correct classificatory scheme to account for lexical items of the lexical-base of Grammar, Generative Grammarians also accept by implication whatever definition of Traditional Grammar makes any lexical item the category it is labelled to be – such as noun, verb, etc. (for if they did not so accept, then the categories would be mere empty labels, and therefore theoretically useless for Grammar).

Lexical categorisation in modern Linguistics

Although Traditional Grammar's categorisation of lexical elements has been recognised, since at least SAUSSURE (1916), to be significantly **problematic**, one important but usually unstated premise of modern Linguistics (which explains neatly Generative Grammar's apparently contradictory adoption of Traditional Grammar's lexical categorisation scheme for its scientific Grammar in spite of Traditional Grammar's theoretical shortcomings in the domain) is that the parts of speech themselves identified by Traditional Grammar are by and large actually **the** categories of Language, but that **the mode of their definition** in Traditional Grammar is essentially flawed, and hence **useless** for identifying lexical items in the conduct of Linguistics science. To remedy the definition situation, **two** basic ways[1] are recognised in much of modern Linguistics for defining (i.e, for specifying the nature of) lexical categories, called ''parts of speech'' by Traditional Grammar. I shall argue in this chapter that both of these two definition modes are fundamentally **unsatisfactory**.

---

1. See FRIES, C.C(1952): *The Structure of English* for an important illustration of a spirited attempt to define lexical categories along these lines in modern Linguistics.

The morphological means definition type

The first is the **morphological** principle mode. Here, the lexical item is defined by the **form** of the word concerned. For example, a morphological definition of the "noun" could identify it by the fact that "the word can be marked for plurality"; thus, **man** is supposedly a noun just because the word can show a change in its form to signal plurality, as is indeed the case with "men" the plural version; and **book** is also supposedly a noun just because the word manifests itself as "books" in the plural form.

The morphological criterion is **unworkable** as a satisfactory definition principle because it has **exceptions** – which show that the criterion inherently cannot cover all the elements of the category targeted. First of all, the criterion may fail even within any given language where it first appeared to work, like English: thus, there are lexical elements like **deer** or **aircraft** which, although considered to be nouns by both Traditional Grammar and modern Linguistics classification schemes, nevertheless do **not** manifest plurality **formally**. Second, the morphological criterion **cannot be universal** – i.e., cannot apply to **all** languages. There are languages, such as Yoruba and Igbo in Nigeria, where the expected or usual situation is that the so-called nouns do **not** show plurality in their forms, while with a language like Bini in Nigeria, the so-called **verbs**, but also nouns, may be formally marked for plurality! Third, the morphological criterion definition type is logically **unworkable** because it applies to the superficial aspects, rather than to the substance, of the lexical item concerned: it is in fact very much like trying to identify who is a soldier by one's uniform; for although soldiers do wear characteristic uniforms, any soldier may sometimes not put on the requisite uniform, while non-soldiers may occasionally be found wearing the uniforms – which explains well why some English so-called adverbs may **not** manifest formally the familiar -ly ending (as is the case with **very** or **soon**) and some other English lexical items which do manifest the familiar –ly ending are generally recognised **not** to be adverbs (such as **family** and **folly**). In short, just as it is **not** the uniform that makes the soldier, so it cannot be the form of the word that makes it this or that lexical category.

The syntactic means definition type

The second basic way in modern Linguistics for defining lexical items is **syntactic**. Here the lexical item is defined by the **position** of the word concerned in relation to other words in a spatio–temporal arrangement in communication. For example, a syntactic definition of the "noun" could characterise it as "any lexical item which manifests itself formally in the **initial position** of a sentence construct". Thus, **cats** as a lexical item would be a noun just because the word involved occurs at the initial position of the sentence numbered "1" below.

1.   Cats   eat   rats.

Like the morphological means type, the syntactic definition principle fails lamentably for characterising the lexical items of the lexicon. First of all, the criterion is unworkable even within a given language, mainly because there is hardly any position in the sentence form which may not be claimed by any of the traditional parts of speech: for example, although the word 'cats' does occur in the first position in my sentence example 1 above (whereby the lexical item is then said to be a noun), the same initial position may also be claimed by virtually any other word associated with other traditional lexical categories – article, adverb, adjective, preposition, etc., as in the sentence examples 2 to 5 below.

1. Cats   eat   rats.
2. The cats ate   rats.
3. Soon the cats will   eat the rats.
4. Hungry   cats   will   eat   rats.
5. In   cats   rats   have enemies.

Secondly, the syntactic criterion for defining lexical categories **cannot be universal** — for there is no fixed word order in sentences construction common to all possible languages. Third, the syntactic means definition principle is **logically unworkable** because, like the morphological principle, it attempts to characterise the lexical item by a superficial quality, rather than by its real nature: it is like trying to identify the cactus by the fact that it grows in the desert; for, although the cactus may indeed be found in the desert, it may also grow elsewhere (like in my garden here in Benin City), while other plants too besides the cactus may be found in the desert. In short, it is **not** the position/location of a plant in the desert that makes the plant a cactus, but rather it is the nature of the cactus (whatever that may be) which makes the plant capable of growing in the desert; similarly it is **not** the position of a lexical form in the sentence construct that defines the category of a lexical item as such, but rather the nature of the lexical item allows that it may manifest itself formally in such or such a position in the construction of a sentence.

The composite features presentation approach

As a rule, Generative Grammarians are **not** really interested in defining lexical categories – whether traditionally, morphologically, or syntactically. The Traditional Grammar classification scheme of 'noun', 'verb', 'preposition', etc. is usually **taken for granted** as it were, but then amplified – as follows. Since 1965, each item in the lexicon, called the **base** of Grammar, is characterised in terms of a set of features. In other words, each lexical item **is** supposedly a composite of features. The features are of **three** types: (i) syntactic, (ii) semantic, and (iii) phonological. Take, for example, the lexical item **dog** of the English language: syntactically, it would be described by the feature ' + noun', semantically, it would be presented with the features '+ noun' '+ animate,' '– human' etc.; phonologically, it would be characterised with the phonetic features of each of the three sound segments that purportedly make up its spoken form.

Far from resolving the lexical categorisation definition problem of Traditional Grammar, Generative Grammar's composite features presentation approach for characterising lexical items actually **compounds the problem**. First, by **refusing** to define the categories of Traditional Grammar which it adopts wholesale, the Generative Grammar approach in effect thereby also **refuses to understand/elucidate** the categories! Second, by using so-called "syntactic" features to characterise lexical items, the approach in effect posits an inherently **false** tenet; for, as we have already seen in this chapter, lexical items do **not** intrinsically have permanent positions which are unique to them in the sentence construct. Third, by using **the same** names of Traditional Grammar's parts of speech for **both** so-called 'syntactic' **and** semantic features (for example, **dog** has the 'syntactic feature' '+ noun' and also the semantic feature '+ noun'; **kill** has the 'syntactic feature' '+ verb', and also the semantic feature '+ verb') the approach to that extent renders intellectually vacuous the lexical categorial labels 'noun', 'verb', 'preposition', 'adverb', etc.

The bi-componential nature of lexical items

To sum up here, Generative Grammar, in its composite features presentation approach, misses tragically the essential point about the nature of the lexical item – and, ultimately of the nature of Language itself as a whole – because of its poor understanding of the true relationship between linguistic form and linguistic meaning. Put succinctly, the lexical item in Generative Grammar is a **tripartite** entity: i.e. (i) it **is** a form (or phonological) unit; (ii) it **is** a meaning (or semantic) unit; and (iii) it **is** a position (or 'syntactic') unit. But this is logically **absurd**: the lexical item is indeed, partly a form unit; it **is** also indeed, partly, a meaning unit; but it **has** (NOT "is") some variable position in textual composition. In other words, the lexical item **is** really partly a form unit and partly a meaning unit – but **nothing else**. Thus, in line with Ferdinand de SAUSSURE's (1916) teachings about the 'sign', the lexical item in Performative Linguistics is a **bi-componential**, NOT a tripartite, Language unit.

Finally, one persistent error which is very characteristic of Generative Grammar, but which is also to be found here and there elsewhere in modern Linguistics, is to assume that the lexical item **as a whole** is a **syntactic** unit – i.e; that the lexical unit **as a whole** is located or locatable in a certain position within a Language construct. It is for this reason, for instance, that the phrase structure and transformation rules of Generative Grammar consistently apply to the lexical item **globally**, making **no** distinction whatsoever between its form part on the one hand and its meaning part on the other hand. In reality, semantic and symbolic units, being different kinds of phenomena, manifest themselves **differently** in Language performance. **It is forms or symbolic units that are 'position – sensitive' as it were**, NOT meanings or semantic units. Consider sentences 6 and 7 for illustration.

6.   John, I know; Ngozi, I don't.
7.   I know John; Ngozi, I don't.

It is the word **John** as a written form which is located in the first position of the sentence construct example 6, and in the third position of the sentence construct example 7; the **semantic fact** itself, that the meaning of the word 'John' is an 'object' remains constant in both sentences 6 and 7, irrespective of the location of its expressing form, the word 'John' – which is really another way of saying that a form may be described in terms of its position (in space or/and in time), but that the meaning of the form is simply mentally **picturable** as a psychological construct and not position-described. It follows from the above demonstration that **the description of texts in Grammar must operate at two separate levels,** as is current standard practice in Performative Grammar – (i) **a semantic level**, which specifies the mentally pictured thought components and relations involved; and (ii) **a symbolic level**, which specifies the time/space positioning of symbolisation components and relations involved.

CHAPTER **6**

GRAMMAR AND PRAGMATICS

CHOMSKY's revolution in Linguistics

Noam CHOMSKY's (1957) **Syntactic Structures** set off the second twentieth-century veritable revolution in Linguistics. The first revolution started with SAUSSURE'S (1916) posthumous *Cours de Linguistique Générale,* which established Linguistics as **an autonomous science discipline** in its own right; the second, CHOMSKY's, has turned Linguistics irrevocably into **an eminent science** – the leader science of central interest to several diverse fields of human preoccupation, such as forensics, museology, and artificial intelligence. The key contribution of CHOMSKY to this development of Linguistics is his **gigantic vision** for the science: where his predecessors were generally satisfied with simply **describing** Language data themselves, CHOMSKY is convinced, and has said so vociferously and repeatedly since 1957, that the goal of Linguistics science must somehow go beyond the mere characterisation of Language substance to **explain** the Language **faculty** itself of the human mind.

Unfortunately, the most damaging weakness of CHOMSKY'S contribution to Linguistics lies in his tools/ methods for attaining his set goal outlined above: they are irremediably flawed. And that is precisely the overall point of this book.

The grammatical tools or methods fail lamentably in two main ways. First, they fail even to describe Language structure satisfactorily; and the reason for this failure is the fundamental misunderstanding by Generative Grammarians of the nature of Language. Second, the tools or methods also fail to explain satisfactorily the Language faculty of the human mind; and the reason for the failure is the problem of so-called psychological reality – i.e, the fact that the claims made about the mind, based on Generative Grammar's account of Language structure, **cannot** reasonably be said to be **really** the case if that mind was **not** taken into account to start with in formulating the structural descriptions from which the psychological explanations were extrapolated.

In the first five chapters of this book, I was concerned with showing **how** Generative Grammar's characterisation of Language was **inherently faulty**. Now in this remaining chapter of the book, I am preoccupied with demonstrating **why** the Generative Grammar scientific paradigm is **inherently useless** for explaining the Language faculty of the human mind.

A psychologically real Grammar must be a Performance Grammar

In the early sixties – that is, after the publication of CHOMSKY'S (1957) *Syntactic Structures*, but before the publication of his *Aspects of the Theory of Syntax* in 1965 – a theoretically very significant claim was being advanced by some Generative Grammarians of the time as an off-shoot benefit of the new Grammar, then called simply 'Transformational Grammar'. The claim was aptly baptised 'the Derivational Theory of Complexity' or DTC for short. According to DTC, given that a generative grammar (as conceived by CHOMSKY, 1957, and exemplified with his then 'Transformational Grammar') supposedly **models the capacity of the mind** even a child of six has to generate a potentially infinite number of a given language's sentences from a finite set of acquired "rules" (i.e., learned processes of construction), then the more **complex** the "rules" of a generative grammar for a given sentence are – that is, the more the number of constructual steps required to **derive** a given sentence – the more difficult the sentence should appear to the mind; and the **longer** therefore for example it should take the language user to construct or comprehend the sentence. Accordingly, Language scholars promptly set about testing the claims; but, although the initial evidence seemed to vindicate DTC, the general consensus before long was that the results of the tests were at best inconclusive and at worst showed DTC to be **false**.

CHOMSKY's response to this theoretic debâcle appeared in his 1965 *Aspects of the Theory of Syntax*, the writing of which could very correctly be said to have been motivated primarily by (i) the Semantic Problem (SP) of his 'Transformational Grammar', then exemplified by the fact that changes in meaning were noticed to have occurred in the derived sentences **after** the supposedly non-meaning-changing transformations had applied to the kernel strings of the sentences; and (ii), the Pragmatic Problem (PP) of the model, exemplified by the DTC theoretic crisis mentioned above. In response to SP, CHOMSKY modified his 'Transformational Grammar', now called 'Transformational Generative Grammar' or simply 'Generative Grammar' as it is nowadays usually called, to, among other things, contain a semantic component – where formerly he had **excluded** Semantics completely from the Grammar. As for PP, CHOMSKY made the theoretically crucial distinction between "competence" and "performance": issues such as those addressed by DTC could **not** reasonably apply to his Grammar, he asserted, because such issues concerned **performance** (i.e., the way Language users actually construct or comprehend sentences), whereas his Generative Grammar, and any Generative Grammar as he then conceived it, was a Grammar of Language **competence** (i.e, of **what** was known, the Language itself) – **not** of its use[1].

---

1 Cf. CHOMSKY, N. (1965 : 9)

> To avoid what has been a continuing misunderstanding, it is perhaps worth while to reiterate that a generative grammar is not a model for a speaker or a hearer. It attempts to characterise in the most neutral possible terms the knowledge of the language that provides the basis for actual use of language by a speaker-hearer. When we speak of a grammar as generating a sentence with a certain structural description, we mean simply that the grammar assigns this structural description to the sentence. When we say that a sentence has a certain derivation with respect to a particular grammar, we say nothing about how the speaker or hearer might proceed, in some practical or efficient way, to construct such a derivation. These questions belong to the theory of language use - the theory of performance. No doubt, a reasonable model of language use will incorporate, as a basic component, the generative grammar that expresses the speaker-hearer's knowledge of the language; but this generative

To draw significant conclusions about the mind on the basis of Grammar (that is, to make serious theoretic claims about the character of the mind based on one's Grammar), it is obvious that one needs a psychologically real Grammar to start with – in other words, one needs a Grammar which models Language structure as it is actually processed (i.e., constructed and comprehended) by that mind. Given that the performance–competence dichotomy was formulated to deal squarely with the pragmatic question of psychological reality (as in DTC, for example), it is also obvious that in the conception of CHOMSKY (1965) **a 'performance Grammar' is a psychologically real Grammar** – in other words, a 'Performance Grammar' in the conception of CHOMSKY (1965) is a Grammar of Language structure as it is actually processed (i.e., constructed and comprehended) by the mind. Now, Generative Grammar is definitely not a performance Grammar according to CHOMSKY (1965); therefore, Generative Grammar (i) is not psychologically real, and therefore (ii) cannot be a correct basis for making serious claims about the Language user's mind.

Context-free Grammars cannot be psychologically real

Generative Grammar is a context-free Grammar – like virtually all serious Grammars, except Performative Grammar, created since linguistic studies began in ancient India some three millennia ago. In a context-free Grammar, Language structures are

---

grammar does not, in itself, prescribe the character or functioning of a perceptual model or a model of speech production.

accounted for **independently of the context** (i.e., independently of contingent circumstances) of their construction or comprehension in real life.

But Language is a context-sensitive phenomenon, however: it is a cultural tool of **real** communities, whose members use it within the constraints of actual conditions of real life. Therefore, any characterisation of Language structure (in other words, any Grammar) which inherently ignores the context-sensitive nature of Language in its elaboration cannot be psychologically real — that is, cannot justifiably claim to constitute a true account of Language as it really is used as a tool in real life by real communities.

As a context-free Grammar, Generative Grammar inherently ignores the context-sensitive nature of Language in its characterisation of Language structure. Therefore, Generative Grammar cannot be psychologically real. Which is why Generative Grammar cannot be a correct basis for making significant claims about the minds of Language users.

A Performance Grammar is also necessarily a Competence Grammar

In formulating the competence-performance dichotomy, CHOMSKY (1965) posited a number of features which purportedly distinguish a Performance Grammar clearly from a Competence Grammar. I argue in this section that the strict distinction between 'performance' and 'competence' as formulated by CHOMSKY (1965) along those lines is actually **not** tenable, and that this fact has deleterious theoretic consequences for the explanatory power of Generative Grammar as a so-called competence Grammar.

A Performance Grammar is, first of all, supposedly concerned with such more or less theoretically unmanageable factors as memory lapse, false starts, slips of the tongue, etc. associated with "the actual use of language in concrete situations"[2], while a Competence Grammar is supposedly **not** so concerned, being purportedly "the underlying system of rules that has been mastered by the speaker-hearer and that he puts to use in actual performance".[3] But this kind of distinction is **false**: a Performance Grammar is **not** really distinguishable from a Competence Grammar by the fact that a Performance Grammar is supposedly sensitive to aberrant contextual factors while a Competence Grammar is not so sensitive. **Any scientific theory** such as a Grammar in Linguistics purports to be, must model **constants**, NOT fortuitous factors; therefore, **both** the so-called Performance Grammar **and** the so-called Competence Grammar must actually **ignore** such arbitrary factors as false starts, memory lapse, distractions, slips of the tongue, etc. to focus on the **characteristic** or inalienable aspects of Language structure. By way of analogy, it would be a sorry model indeed of building engineering which preoccupied itself seriously with such freak factors as that the builder happens to have a cold, that his trowel could fall from his hands on the ninth floor of the building, or that it was cloudy on a particular morning – instead of being

---

2. see CHOMSKY, N. (1965: 4)

3. Ibid,

essentially concerned with the compositional character of the building itself.

A Performance Grammar is **not** distinguishable either from a Competence Grammar with the claim that a Performance Grammar supposedly models the **use** of Language "in concrete situations"[4] while a Competence Grammar supposedly models the **knowledge** of Language (structure) that one "puts to use in actual performance."[5] A model of the **use** of Language **cannot be a Grammar** at all, because **any** Grammar models Language **structure** NOT Language use; therefore, a Performance Grammar, whatever it may be correctly specified to be, **cannot be** a model of Language **use**. On the other hand, a model of one's knowledge of Language structure, which supposedly defines a 'Competence Grammar' according to CHOMSKY (1965), is what **every** Grammar in fact is; therefore, a Performance Grammar, whatever else it may correctly be specified to be, is also necessarily a Competence Grammar – whereby the expression 'Competence Grammar' as 'the model of one's knowledge of Language structure' becomes intellectually vacuous.

It might seem reasonable to posit that a Competence Grammar is perhaps the model or characterisation of the knowledge of Language structure as it is **stored** in the Language user, **waiting** to be **used**, while a Performance Grammar is perhaps the model or characterisation of the knowledge of Language structure **actually put to use**. But the knowledge of Language structure "waiting to be used" **cannot be different**

---
4. CHOMSKY, N. (1965: 4)
5. Ibid,

from the knowledge of Language structure.''actually put to use'': indeed, it is **the same** knowledge which is **made manifest** in use (i.e., in 'performance') that has to be **stored** (i.e; in 'competence') Thus understood, then, performance is really actualised competence while competence is potential performance – the knowledge itself modelled by Grammar being essentially **the same**, whether in use or waiting to be used.

What, then, remains of theoretic importance in the performance-competence dichotomy as formulated by CHOMSKY (1965)? The **only viable distinction** between a so-called Competence Grammar and a so-called Performance Grammar lies in the notion of psychological reality as we have already seen in this chapter: a Performance Grammar models Language structure as it is processed by the mind in real life, whereby it is correctly said, to be ''psychologically real'', while a Competence Grammar does **not** model Language structure as it is processed by the mind in real life, whereby it is correctly said **not** to be ''psychologically real''. Furthermore, it is worth noting here that context-sensitiveness is a crucial but **insufficient** condition by itself for psychological reality: thus, a psychologically real Grammar (i.e., one which models Language structure as it is actually processed by the mind) is necessarily context-sensitive, but a Grammar may conceivably be context-sensitive, as in the field-work data collection exercises of American Structuralist Linguistics, without necessarily being psychologically real. If, therefore, Generative Grammar is truly the ''Competence Grammar'' which CHOMSKY (1965) claims it is, then it cannot but be devoid of psychological reality; hence it is fundamentally **incapable** of explaining the Language faculty of the human mind.

Language text and Language context

The explanatory **inadequacy** of Generative Grammar shows up quite clearly also in its total inability to handle the pragmatic problem of relating Language context, the subject matter of Pragmatics, to Language text, the subject matter of Grammar, within Linguistics. And that is the issue I wish to address hereafter.

Now as twenty-first century Linguistics begins, I believe that it is essential for the development of Linguistics as a leader science that Linguists should first review and resolve as satisfactorily as possible with insights available the major stumbling blocks of Linguistic Theory in the twentieth century. One of such major problems – I would say **the** problem – is the interface between Pragmatics and Grammar. What, exactly, is the relationship between Pragmatics and Grammar? More precisely, to what extent (if at all) are pragmatic considerations really pertinent for grammatical descriptions?

In effect, up to now, a clear distinction has generally been drawn in modern Linguistics between Microlinguistics[6] or Grammar, the study of the structure of Language (traditionally understood as the structure of sentence units, but actually the structure of **any** Language units, including those larger than the sentence) on the one hand, and Pramalinguistics or Pragmatics, the study of Language use.[7] The underlying need for this crucial

---

6. See LYONS, J. (1981 : 36).
7. While recognising that the definition of 'Pragmatics' remains controversial (see LYONS, 1981 : 171 as well as the goals of the International Pragmatics Association as stated in its *Pragmatics* journal

distinction between matters of Language structure and those of Language use was specially felt from about the last quarter of the twentieth century with what I have called "The Pragmaticist Movement"[8], which has since resulted in the rise of Pragmatics as a full-blown subdiscipline of Linguistics. The movement attracted the very many prominent Linguists who embraced the spirit of the then new Language use doctrine from Philosophy first articulated by the Philosopher J.L. AUSTIN and later by another Philosopher, J.R., SEARLE. The Linguists shared the conviction that there is much more to Linguistics than Generative Grammar's apparent obsession with Language structure[9] – or, as put succinctly in Performative Linguistics, that "the nature of Language is more than just a matter of the structure of Language" but also concerns the use of Language. In this modern linguistic dichotomy between Grammar and Pragmatics, Language Acts Theory[10], the characterisation of sentence constructs specifically of Language performance, is understood to be part of Pragmalinguistic(s) or Pragmatic(s) Theory, which is the characterisation of Language performance in general.

---

for examples), I expect that this my definition is one which is most likely to be accepted by the overwhelming majority of scholars in the field.

8. See UWAJEH, M.K.C. (2000a): "Main Advances in Language Acts Theory" Forthcoming in JOLAN.

9 See LAKOFF, R.T. (1993); MEY, J.L (1994): and GOATLY, A. (1994) for useful discussions.

10 I use the expression 'Language Acts' instead of 'speech acts' (as in SEARLE, 1969 for a classic example) since Philosophers (notably J.L. AUSTIN and J.R. SEARLE) started teaching Linguists about such Language phenomena because, although speech (i.e, spoken Language) **is** indeed Language of course, Language is **not necessarily** speech. See UWAJEH, M.K.C. (1996a, 2000a, 2000b, 2001a and 2002) for other justifications of the use of 'Language/Linguistic Acts'.

But, is a clear distinction possible between Pragmatics and Grammar? In other words, can the contextual factors of Pragmatics be justifiably separated from the textual features of Grammar within Linguistics? In these last sections of this chapter, I not only argue that such a strict separation is **not** tenable but I also show the correct relationship between Pragmatics and Grammar.

The importance of context in Grammar

To start with, let me now advance here the thesis that the contextual issues of Pragmatics **are indispensable** for dealing with the structural matters of Grammar in the proper conduct of grammatical descriptions. This is a revolutionary thesis indeed, in the sense that follows: up to now, it has generally been assumed that one's Grammar may electively be **either** context-free (as with CHOMSKY'S 1965, etc. so-called "Competence Grammar" which his Generative Grammar purportedly is) **or** context-sensitive (as with what CHOMSKY 1965, etc. called a "Performance Grammar," which his Generative Grammar decidedly is **not**) and still be a satisfactory characterisation of Language nevertheless; but my claim here is that **a context-free Grammar cannot ever be a satisfactory characterisation of Language structure because Language structure features cannot be accounted for correctly without obligatory reference to contextual factors**. I support this claim hereafter by examining, for an illustrative example, the issue of the illocutionary categorisation of sentences in Grammar.

It seems so perfectly reasonable to almost constitute a truism that a sentence of any imaginable language must show **somehow** by its structure whether it is, for example, a declarative sentence, an interrogative sentence, or an imperative. In this regard, English sentences similar in construction pattern to sentence 1 below would be declarative, those similar to sentence example 2 would be interrogative, and those similar to sentence example 3 would be imperative.

1. You will attend the meeting, Henry.

2. Did Henry attend the meeting?

3. Attend the meeting, Henry!

All mainstream linguistic description frameworks since antiquity – from ancient Indian and Greek linguistic studies to modern Structuralist and Generative Linguistics especially – have endorsed this neat structure-based approach to sentences classification. I claim that it is a **wrong** approach to sentences classification in particular and to linguistic analysis generally – as explained hereunder. Consider, for my illustrative discussion, the following possible English sentence.

4. Burn down Central Bank, man!

One might readily infer from its structural similarity to sentence example 3 that this is a command or imperative sentence.

3. Attend the meeting, Henry!

However, supposing in actual fact that this sentence was a construct transmitted from a disgruntled Nigerian complaining about the ridiculously low value of the national currency (the naira) vis-à-vis the American dollar, in answer to the following question from a television station reporter:

5. What would be your first executive action, Sir, if you had the singular good fortune to become the President of this Giant of Africa?

2. Burn down Central Bank, man!

Then it would be immediately obvious that we are dealing with a declarative sentence. Similarly, one could easily think, without any further index to go by than the sentence structure itself, that the sentence example 6 below must be an interrogative sentence – given its apparent structural similarity to sentence example 2.

6. Are you mad?

2. Did Henry attend the meeting?

But I have to date coincidentally had as neighbours here in Benin City two different families in which the sentence token in question is a routine way whereby the mothers concerned express their exasperation in reaction to some mischief or the other of the children's. From observing the actual situations of usage, I have come to realise that the mothers are in fact **declaring** to the children with the sentence token that they the children **are** "mad" (in behaving the way they have done), and **not** seeking to find out whether indeed the children are mad. The sentence concerned is thus, under the circumstances here depicted, clearly an assertion or declarative, NOT a question or interrogative – in spite of its structure.

Consider, too, sentence example 7 below.

7.   You will shoot me, Fred.

One could easily think, without any contextual index to go by, that the sentence construct must be a declarative, going again by the structural pattern of my sentence example 1 above.

1.   You will attend the meeting, Henry.

However, supposing the sentence happened to be a construct transmitted from a mafioso to his friend in crime who he suddenly realises is taking him away for execution, on the orders of their boss; and supposing furthermore that Fred's immediate reply during their terminal ride was the sentence example 8 below.

7.   You will shoot me, Fred.

8.   Yes, Greg; sorry things have to end this way.

Then it would become obvious that Greg's apparent statement sentence is in fact a question or interrogative sentence construct.

Consider further sentence example 9 below for another illustration of the very important theoretic claim here being made in Performative Linguistics regarding the apparent uselessness of the structure criterion for the illocutionary classification of sentences.

9.   May I ask you a question?

Is this sentence a question, given its structural similarity to my sentence example 2?

2. Did Henry attend the meeting?

Firstly, the sentence token concerned might of course be a question – as is evident from the following exchange:

9. May I ask you a question?

10. Yes, you may.

In the context, the communicatee has fairly obviously interpreted the communicator's illocutive intent for sentence example 9 as a desire to be informed about something. Secondly, the sentence could be a request (i.e, a polite imperative) and **not** an interrogative construct – as could be evident from the following exchange.

9. May I ask you a question?

11. Go ahead, please.

Thirdly, it could be an "illocutively double-barrelled expression"[11] – here, both question and request imperative – when the response of the communicatee[12] to the sentence example 9 happened to be something like sentence example 12.

---

11. See UWAJEH, M.K.C. (1996 : 98)
12. I am obviously **not** implying with my illustrative examples throughout this section that a (linguistic) response by the communicatee to a specific sentence construct is the contextual determinant as to the illocutive

9. May I ask you a question?
12. Yes, go ahead.

Given that the various demonstrations above have of course been pointing to the crucial role of context in the correct illocutionary categorisation of sentences, am I therefore claiming that sentence structure is completely irrelevant for categorising sentences illocutively? **NO**, that is **not** my position. It is actually true that certain sentence constructs structure types do **tend to** reflect some particular illocutionary classification categories. Indeed, were the situation essentially otherwise, 'Language' would to that extent be a chaotic phenomenon, and corresponding linguistic communication fundamentally inefficient as a social tool.

Generally speaking, however, sentential structures **by themselves**, although quite useful as I have just admitted for **suggesting** the communicator's illocutive intent, are yet an **insufficient** guide to that effect: communication context itself is the **absolute guarantee** as to the communicator's exact illocutive intent. Thus, a sentence's structure *per se* is only a **rough** index pointing to the specific illocutive category of that sentence: the structure is necessarily supplemented by, even **overridden** by, contextual facts – which usually go a long way to direct and focalise the intelligent **guesses** of the communicatee's (that his/her linguistic decodings essentially are anyway) regarding the

---

category of that particular sentence: I have merely demonstrated that such a clue can suggest to us the true illocutive intent of the language communicator, and therefore how the communicator's sentence may be illocutively classified by the Linguist - whatever the structure available.

communicator's exact illocutionary intentions.[13] Ultimately, the case for a context-based approach to the illocutionary categorisation of sentences rests on this inescapable logic that **whereas a language communicator does not necessarily intend the illocutionary force which his/her language construct structure alone would have us believe he/she intends, the contextual factors of that language act inevitably do guarantee the illocutionary intents he/she has imposed on his/her linguistic communication, whatever the structure of his/her sentence construct**.

Given the central thesis above highlighted and discussed in this section, it seems to me that the correct approach to the illocution-level categorisation of sentences is **not** to assert dogmatically that such or such types of sentence pattern are such or such illocution types; but, instead, that with such or such an illocutive intent, as deducible from the actual contextual facts of the Language communication act, then such or such structures are **likely to reflect it** for this or that given language. In short, the actual particular communication context of a communicator's communication, **NOT** that communicator's sentence's structure by itself, is the **ultimate** basis for ascertaining the communicator's communicated illocutive intent for his/her sentence construct.

---

13. Since the communicatee's decoding of the communicator's language performance amounts to guesses (howbeit intelligent) of the communicator's communicated intent(s), it goes without saying that the communicatee could still be mistaken about the communicator's exact illocutive intent in spite of all the available contextual cues and clues of a given linguistic communication.

The pragmatic criterion of communication context is also even crucial for **sentence structure typification** too (in addition to the sentence's illocutionary force specification, as we have just seen above). Consider the following sentences for illustration.

13   My friends and I are sore losers.

4.   Burn down Central Bank, man!

9.   May I ask you a question?

14. Are you alright?

That sentence construct example 13 above could have an illocutionary force of a **warning** (when addressed to the boxing opponent of a mafioso protégé, say) rather than that of an assertion is actually to say that this sentence example structure could become that of (i.e., become a structure used for expressing) a warning, not that of an assertion; similarly, the structure of sentence example 4 could be that of an assertion not an order, given an assertion illocutionary force; the structure of sentence example 9 could be that of a request, not of a question, given a request illocutionary force; and the structure of sentence example 14 could be correctly said to be that of a wish, not of a question, given a wish illocutionary force. Since (as I have already shown in this section) a sentence construct's illocutionary force is context-dependent, and the typification of sentence structure itself (as just demonstrated in this paragraph) does depend on the illocutionary force of the language act concerned, then sentence structure specification depends ultimately on the communication context of the sentence's production.

Beyond Generative Grammar

Admitted, then, that the Pragmatics criterion of communication context is indispensable for the structural description of Language in Grammar as I have now shown, what is the exact relationship in Linguistics between Pragmatics, the study of Language communication context or use, and Grammar, the study of Language communication text or structure? The hypothesis in Performative Linguistics is that **Language structure is determined by Language use**.

This hypothesis is of course already vindicated by the fact demonstrated in this chapter that communication context is indispensable for the structural description of Language. If the hypothesis is found to be universally correct, it would follow without doubt that **Grammar, the study of Language text or structure, is dependent on Pragmatics, the study of Language context or use**. This would dissolve irrevocably the strict distinction maintained to date between Grammar and Pragmatics – for it would imply that Grammar could never be properly conducted in Linguistics without strict reference to Pragmatics. In that case, we should surely witness the demise in twenty-first century Linguistics of context-free Grammars in general and of Generative Grammar in particular as the most influential example to date of context-free Grammars.

CONCLUSION: CHAOS THEORY IN LINGUISTICS

In 1977, at the Université de Montréal, I began to work seriously for a Unified Linguistic Theory to account comprehensively for the similarities I thought I saw common to **all** types of simplified language – from baby talk and foreigner talk to zoo language and telegram language; etc. According to my premise, it was theoretically trivial simply to **list** the features themselves observed – as had hitherto been attempted for, notably, child and pidgin languages individually; what was needed, the real issue of academic interest I argued, should be to **explain** just **why** those particular features always surfaced in the various types of simplified language. In other words, one needed to determine what indeed those observed common features could tell us about the nature of Language which perhaps we did not already know or even suspect. That quest (and the subject matter of my doctoral thesis incidentally) turned out to become the most intellectually demanding task I have ever undertaken: it led me to re-think the discipline of Linguistics generally, and, in particular, to create a new, performance theory of Language structure which I named **Performative Grammar**.

With hindsight, I now know that I also encountered the problem of **chaos** for the first time during that research in Linguistics, without being aware of the name or theory at the time. What I was confronted with in specific terms was the perfectly annoying realisation that there seemed to be no rule-governed way of characterising satisfactorily sentence structures of (simplified) language in terms of the linguistic parameters of 'old' (or 'known') information and 'new' (or 'current') information: that is, I could **not** correctly assert, for example, that in any given language's sentence text the subject component invariably conveyed old information, while the corresponding predicate component conveyed predictably the new information. Now, a satisfactory resolution of this matter was of paramount importance to me then because a crucial consequence of my research into the nature of simplified language was that I had come to understand the old and new information dichotomy to be the overriding basis for describing the entire sentence structure, and that all other types of structural description – such as those of subject-predicate or noun phrase and verb phrase distinctions, or head and modifying constituents categorisations, etc. – must be subordinated to the old-new information divisions of the sentence, from its immediate to its ultimate lexical constituents. Unlike Wallace CHAFE (in his book *Meaning and the Structure of Language*, 1970), whom I admired immensely and was very reluctant to contradict, I had discovered that even for such a very simple sentence as 'the box is empty' you could **not** (i.e., in a rule-governed way) assert correctly that such or such an immediate structural component is always the old or the new information constituent: 'the box' can be the new information, while 'is empty' becomes the old information constituent, if the sentence is produced, for instance, as a normal response to the question "What do you say is empty?"; on the other hand, for the same sentence example, 'the box' could also be the old information constituent and 'is empty' now the new information component, if, for illustration, both the communicator (i.e, the producer of the sentence concerned in real life) and the communicatee (i.e, the addressee of the sentence produced in real life) had been looking for a certain box (presumably full of valuables), which the communicator of the given sentence found first and used the sentence in question for announcing (truly or falsely) the nature of his find.

The more I wrestled with this problem of **unpredictability** just highlighted above – i.e., with the indeterminacy principle that confounded the seeker of which sentence constituents types always bore what information type – the more obvious it became to me that **context** (of language communication) was the **constant** that unfailingly determined which sentence constituent did convey what type of information: that is, to specify which constituents were respectively old and new information parts, you simply first ascertain the circumstances which gave rise to the sentence as a *bona fide* communication act product in real life. Paradoxically, this realisation, far from satisfying me, constituted a very alarming discovery indeed that threw me into pangs of confusion.

You see, essentially all linguistic studies – since the priestly caste of Ancient India discovered them, since the ancient Greek sages laid their foundation for Western civilisation, and since the Swiss linguistic genius Ferdinand de SAUSSURE created an autonomous science therefrom at the beginning of the twentieth century – had been predicated on the axiom that one did **not** have to bother about the circumstances of the production of a sentence (that is, about its context) before describing successfully the structure of that sentence. Communication context was generally recognised as a marginal factor in Language characterisation, and sentence structures were supposed to be describable more or less automatically, without reference to the communication situations of their emission. The acme of this mechanistic approach to the characterisation of Language in Linguistics science has been, with its seductive formalisation apparatus especially at its inception, Noam CHOMSKY's revolutionary Generative Grammar: in such a theoretical framework, Grammar (that is Language structure characterisation) is said to be essentially context-**free** – **independent** of context, that is. What alarmed me so much was therefore that my research was leading me to the diametrically **opposite** view to that hallowed by hundreds of years of linguistic studies tradition, the opposite view that any Grammar purporting to be realist (i.e., any Grammar laying down serious claims to contributing intellectually significant facts to the academic community about the true nature of Language) must be context-**sensitive** (or context-dependent, in other words). Informed somehow about the direction my work was taking me, Professor Antonio QUERIDO of the Université de Montréal asked me at the time apropos my ambitious theoretical claims whether I was not afraid of making them (so early in my academic career). I remember replying that I **was** afraid indeed, and would really have preferred not to be obliged to make them, but that the facts were too compelling for me not to articulate. As the Biologist Jacques MONOD aptly put it in his book, *Le Hasard et la Nécessité* (1970), modesty fits the scholar himself, **not** the ideas in him – which he has the duty to defend resolutely.

The more immediate reason, however, for my initial discomfiture before the recognition of the crucial importance of context for a realist Grammar was as follows. As everyone knows, context is characteristically **unpredictable:** for that very simple sentence 'The box is empty' again, this means that we can never say with certainty which part is the new information or old information constituent, unless we happen to witness a communication situation wherein the sentence constitutes an appropriate linguistic communication product. Now, since context is unpredictable, I was in effect making an unpredictable factor a crucial component of my linguistic theory. Hence my worry; for, given that science as I knew it had all along been based on the predictable, repeatable, or constant, was I not unwittingly turning Linguistics into an impossible science with the unpredictability factor of context as its bedrock? Without knowing it then, I had encountered for the first time, in Linguistics, the problem of **chaos**.

The solution to this problem in Linguistics dawned on me in a public park near the Côte des Neiges section of Montréal where I did the best of my brainwork at the time. I suddenly realised with a flash of insight that the oft-vaunted creativity in, or dynamic nature of, Language was reflected precisely in the apparent disorder I had stumbled upon and that I found so overwhelmingly disconcerting. A deterministic theory, which purportedly predicted with exactitude the occurrence of every structural feature of Language, could never truly account for this apparently non-rule-governed Language Faculty in us, because such a logical framework is mechanistic in essence and we Language users are certainly **not** automatons. Once I had fully accepted the just-mentioned fact about the dynamic essence of Language with its implications, several things fell into place instantly, and I grasped with a breathtaking clarity the true nature of Language. I saw, for one, that the order manifest in the structure of Language is truly understandable only in terms of **probabilities**, NOT certainties. Thus, for illustration, given some particular information particularity to be transmitted, any one of several different structural strategies, within the same language or across many different languages, **could** (more or less probably) be used by the communicator to convey it; and it is therefore methodologically fruitless to expect absolute certainty regarding which one exactly of those structural strategies the communicator will always adopt for every specific communication act. In this new perspective, Grammar becomes a characterisation of what language structural organisations are available which **may** (more or less probably) serve what communication functions in given contexts (types) – instead of a description, generative or otherwise, of 'frozen', context-independent Language textual structures which have hardly anything to do with the realities of communication. In other words, the dynamic nature of Language lies essentially in the communicator's relative **freedom of choice** to adopt any one of several structural constructions he/she deems fit to serve the contextual exigency confronting him/her for every specific communication act; or, Language structure is the **product** of the communicator's creative **choice** of units and patterns of Language elements to serve specific contextual communication functions; or, 'Language is an intelligent performance', as I would nowadays put it succinctly in Performative Linguistics.

Since the nineteen eighties, my firm conviction about the crucial role of communication context in the characterisation of Language has led me to insights that should be of interest to both Linguists and non-Linguists. Within Linguistics, for example, my so-called illocutionary theory of sentence categorisation postulates that the classical structure-based, context-free approach to sentence categorisation is, as we have seen in this book, fundamentally inadequate: the classification of sentences into statements, requests, questions, etc. **is**, too, context-sensitive like the classification of texts into new or old information constituents, according to this my theory. Within and outside

Linguistics, I share with other scientists the pressing need to find a new, adequate frame of reference to replace the classical Newtonian determinism by which Science has been conducted until very recent times. If, as has become increasingly inescapable to the scientific community, Chaos Theory is here to stay, then it is **not** quite satisfactory enough to state, as is currently done in scientific circles, that beyond the apparent disorder (wherefore the name 'Chaos'), so far observed in the physical universe as we know it, some kind of order underlies nature. On the contrary, we need a new, conceptually clear and intellectually illuminating portraiture of the exact character of this strange cosmological principle (called 'Chaos') that is neither completely deterministic as hitherto thought since Isaac NEWTON'S universal laws nor yet totally fortuitous, as the scientifically naive might nowadays conclude from the name 'Chaos'.

I myself suggest that the expression **empirical context** actually fits best the principle now known to govern our understanding of the universe – NOT 'chaos', which although so far popular with the scientific community (no doubt because it has a high mnemonic value – like 'quarks', and 'charms', etc.) is nevertheless conceptually **misleading** and a misnomer for the phenomenon being designated, since it tends to be understood in terms of absolute disorder – or at least to suggest such disorder. By 'empirical context', I propose that the nature of a phenomenon – that is, what a thing really is – can be properly understood only with reference to the complex of contingent factors that have brought about the observed phenomenon: in other words, every phenomenon of the universe may be properly described only as a 'contextual event'. 'Empirical context' as a notion helps to appreciate soundly and unify several, sometimes apparently irreconcilable, theories of modern science: for example, the nature of the phenomenon in the mechanics of Albert EINSTEIN's Relativity Theory (concerning the principle that only relative, not absolute, motion can be observed in the universe) is indeed significantly contingent on the contextual variable of **who** is observing the contextual event of motion; and for the phenomenon in the quantum mechanics of HEISENBERG's Indeterminacy Theory (concerning the principle whereby it is impossible to measure with strict precision both the position and momentum of a particle simultaneously), or even for the phenomenon in the quantum mechanics of BOHR'S Complementarity Theory (concerning the principle whereby an experiment on one aspect of a system of atomic dimensions may destroy the possibility of learning about a 'complementary' aspect of the same system), EINSTEIN need not have complained publicly in exasperation that "God does not play dice" with nature, because the methodologically sensible thing to do in line with my principle of empirical context is to consider as **two**, NOT one, **different** contextual events the particle's simultaneously indeterminate position and momentum (of HEISENBERG'S Indeterminacy Principle) on the one hand as well as the system's 'complementary' aspects (of BOHR'S Complementarity Principle) on the other hand.

To conclude, the empirical context principle not only makes good sense of the apparently baffling character of our universe currently described by scientists as 'chaos' but should also especially help to bridge the intellectual gap between Science and Philosophy. Up to now, the hallmark of Science was the analysis and description of the **constituency** of phenomena: thus, a given molecule of chemical substance was so many atomic elements bonded in some specific arrangement; a given atom of matter was its component physical particles linked to one another in some relationship; and a given sentence of Language texture was a composition of so many interrelated phrase units; and so on and so forth. It is this mechanistic empirical view of phenomena that I have challenged and shown to be fundamentally inadequate: **the nature of a phenomenon is more than a matter of the make-up of that phenomenon;** that make-up can in fact only be properly understood in terms of the phenomenon's empirical context. By thus extending the preoccupation of Science beyond the phenomenon's make-up or structure, certain issues which were formerly the preserve of Philosophy now become respectable in Science as well. Hitherto, in order to characterise the universe, Science excluded questions such as those regarding 'who?' (if anybody) made the universe, and 'why?' (if for any reason at all) it was made. Henceforth, the principle of empirical context makes such questions unavoidable in Science. There is, of course, no guarantee that we shall find satisfactory answers to any, some, or all of those kinds of questions; but we scientists should no longer refuse to ask them for fear of being unable to answer them....

WORKS CITED

ABDULLAHI, M.D. (1992): "Language, National Unity and Democratisation Process: The Case for a New Writing" Keynote address delivered at the 1992 Annual Conference of the Linguistic Association of Nigeria (LAN) : University of Abuja; 2-5 November, 1992.

AUSTIN, J.L. (1962): *How to Do Things with Words* Edited by URMSON, J.O. Oxford University Press.

BLOOMFIELD, L. (1933): *Language.* New York: Holt, Rinehart and Winston.

BULLOCK, A. and
STALLYBRASS: O. (eds, 1977): *The Harper Dictionary of Modern Thought.* New York: Harper and Row.

CHAFE, W.L. (1970): *Meaning and the Structure of Language.* Chicago: University of Chicago Press.

CHOMSKY, N. (1957): *Syntactic Structures.* The Hague: Mouton.

CHOMSKY, N. (1962): "Current Issues in Linguistic Theory" In FODOR J.A. and KATZ, J.J. (eds; 1964): *The Structure of Language.* Englewood Cliffs, N.J.: Prentice-Hall Inc.

CHOMSKY, N. (1965): *Aspects of the Theory of Syntax.* Cambridge, Mass.: M.I.T. Press.

CHOMSKY, N. (1975): *Reflections on Language.* New York: Pantheon.

CHOMSKY, N. (1995): "Bare Phrase Structure" In WEBELHUTH, G. (ed; 1995): *Government and Binding Theory and the Minimalist Program.* Oxford: Blackwell Publishers Ltd.

COULMAS, F. (1990): "A Review of COOPER, C.R. and GREENBAUM, S. (eds; 1986): *Studying Writing. Linguistic Approaches*". In *Linguistics*, 28 (1): 173 – 175.

FRIES, C.C. (1952): *The Structure of English*. New York: Harcourt Brace and World.

GOATLY, A. (1994): "Register and the Redemption of Relevance Theory: The Case of Metaphor". In *Pragmatics*, 4 (2): 139–181.

HEFFNER, R.M.S. (1952): *General Phonetics*. University of Wisconsin Press

LAKOFF, R.T. (1993): "Lewis Carroll: Subversive Pragmaticist". In *Pragmatics*, 3 (4): 367 – 385.

LINDEN, E. (1976): *Apes, Man and Language* London and New York: Pengiun.

LYONS, J. (1981): *Language and Linguistics. An Introduction.* Cambridge: Cambridge University Press.

MATTHEWS, P.H. (1979): *Generative Grammar and Linguistic Competence.* London: George Allen and Unwin.

MEY, J.L. (1994): "How to Do Good Things with Words. A Social Pragmatics for Survival". In *Pragmatics*, 4 (2): 239–263.

MONOD, J. (1970): *Le Hasard et la Nécessité.* Paris: Editions du Seuil.

NWACHUKWU, P.A. (1985): "Inherent Complement Verbs in Igbo". In *JOLAN*, No 3: 61 – 74.

OGDEN, C.K. and
RICHARDS, I.A. (1923): *The Meaning of Meaning.* London: Routledge and Kegan Paul.

PEARSON, B.L. (1977): *Introduction to Linguistic Concepts.* New York: Alfred A. Knopf.

ROBINS, R. H. (1979): *A Short History of Linguistics.* London: Longman.

RUMBAUGH, D.M. (1977): *Language Learning by A Chimpanzee. THE LANA PROJECT.* New York: Academic Press

SAPIR, E. (1921): *Language.* New York: Harcourt Brace and World.

de SAUSSURE, F. (1916): *Cours de Linguistique Générale.* Paris: Payot.

SEARLE, J.R. (1969): *Speech Acts.* Cambridge: Cambridge University Press.

SWEET, H. (1901): *A Primer of Phonetics.* Oxford: Clarendon Press.

TERRACE, H.S. (1979): *NIM, A Chimpanzee Who Learned Sign Language.* New York: Washington Square Press.

TIME-LIFE BOOKS (1973): "The Gift of Language"; Chapter 4 in *The First Men (pp. 97–110):* New York. Time Inc,

UWAJEH, M.K.C. (1979): *Structures Syntaxiques du Deuxième Registre*. Thèse de Doctorat; Département de Linguistique, Université de Montréal.

UWAJEH, M.K.C. (1990): "A Review of D.S. CLARKE Jr.s *Principles of Semiotic*" In *Communication and Cognition*, 23 (1):111 – 116.

UWAJEH, M.K.C. (1993): "Communication Context" in Translation" In *TURJUMAN*, 2 (1):117 – 128.

UWAJEH, M.K.C. (1993): *Teach Your Child to Write* Benin City: Supreme Ideal Publishers.

UWAJEH, M.K.C. (1994):. "The Case for a Performative Translatology" In *PERSPECTIVES: Studies in Translatology*, 1994; 2: 245–257

UWAJEH, M.K.C. (1996): "Is 'May I ask you a question?' a Question?" In *Pragmatics*, 6(1): 89–109.

UWAJEH, M.K.C. (1996): "Meaning in Performative Translatology" In *TURJUMAN*, 5(1): 59-80.

UWAJEH, M.K.C. (1996): "Literal Meaning in Performative Translatology" In *PERSPECTIVES: Studies in Translatology;* 1996, 2: 189-201

UWAJEH, M.K.C. (1996): "Translation in African Education" In *African Journal of Education,* 1(1): 81-92

UWAJEH, M.K.C. (1999): "Translation and African Development" In *PERSPECTIVES: Studies in Translatology;*7(1): 109- 122

UWAJEH, M.K.C. (2000): "Main Advances in Language Acts Theory". Forthcoming in *JOLAN*.

UWAJEH, M.K.C. (2000): "Indication, Representation, and Intentionality: Another Reply to SEARLE'S Critics" in *RALL 6 (1): 88-116.*

UWAJEH, M.K.C. (2001): "Linguistic Acts and Semantic Facts" In *Kiabara*, 7(1): 83-94.

UWAJEH, M.K.C. (2001): "The Task of the Translator Revisited in Performative Translatology" In *Babel*, 47(3): 228-247.

UWAJEH, M.K.C. (2002): "Translation Studies in Pragmatics" Forthcoming in *Kiabara*.

WHORF, B.L. (1956): *Language, Thought and Reality*. Cambridge, Mass. M.I.T. Press.

Index

ABDULLAHI, 103
Acoustic Phonetics, 101
active
— competence, 31-33
— Language competence, 31-33
adjective, 109, 113
adverb, 109, 111, 113, 115
Albert EINSTEIN's Relativity Theory, 145
alphabetic writing system, 97
alphabets (written letters stand for phonemes of specific languages), 94
American structuralist linguistics, 126
ancient linguistic studies, 63
anthropocentric statements, 90
A-P, 9
arbitrary
— factors, 124
— relationship, 29
— symbols, 90
article, 109, 113
articulatory
— organs, 41
Articulatory-Perceptual, 9
articulatory phonetics, 101-102
artifacts
— behavioural, 34
— material, 34
— mental, 34

artistic expression, 18
Aspects of the Theory of Syntax, 8, 120
atomic elements, 145
aural (hearing) symbolisation, 98
AUSTIN, J. L. 128
automatons, 142
autonomous science discipline, 118
auxiliary
— constituent language, 71
— lexical item, 71

baby talk, 138
base, 108, 114
basic constituents, 34
behavioural artifacts, 34
Benin City, 20, 113. 131
Beyond Generative Grammar, 137
bi-componential nature of lexical items, 115-117
Bini, 31, 171
biological priority, 95-96
biologist, 141
BLOOMFIELD, 101
BOHR, 145
BOHR's complementarity Principle, 145
BOND, James, 76-77
Braille writing, 98
building blocks, 108

BULLOCK, A., 35
cactus, 113
CHAFE, Wallace, 139
Chaos, 138, 145
- problem of, in Linguistics, 142
- Theory, 144
- Theory in Linguistics, 138-146
characteristic, 30
characterisation of Language, 16
charms, 144
cheremes, 99
Cheremics, 100
Cheretics, 100
Cheresemics, 100
cheric
- Phrase Syntax, 107
- Sentence Syntax, 107
- Text Syntax, 107
cherics, 99-100
Cherology, 107
Cheromorphology, 107
child language, 138
CHOMSKY N., 8-9, 15-16, 81-83, 89, 118-123, 125-126, 129, 141
CHOMSKY's Revolution in Linguistics, 118-119
C-I, 9
classification schemes, 111
classificatory scheme, 109
clausal/sentential constructs, 56
code, 21
colour spectrum, 66
command sentence, 130
Commonwealth of Nations, 28
communicable preoccupations of Language, 34
communicate indirectly, 23
communicatee, 6, 17, 19, 21, 25-27, 31-32, 53, 133-135

communicating
- beings, 21
- individual, 21
- parties, 21
communication
- by representation, 21
- competence, 16
- context, 3, 35, 52, 136-137, 140
- free, 2
- role of, 143
- exigencies, 3
- function, 71
- of, 18
- of Language, 17
- general means of, 21
- indicational means of, 4
- intent, 19-22
- indicated, 20
- intention, 20
- Linguistic means of, 22
- means, 19-21
- indicator, 20
- of, 4, 17
- mode, 95
- needs, 95
- of experiences, 11, 24
- representational means of, 4
- setting, 20
- situation, 142
- situations consonant
- skills, 16, 23, 33
- specialised means of, 4, 21
- speed of, 6
- tool, 16
- tools, 19, 27
- without Language, 17
communicative
- actions, 19
- character of language, 17
- constraints, 4
- constructs, 4
- exigencies, 4

156

- power, 18
- rules, 94
communicator, 6, 17, 19, 26, 32, 53, 134-135, 140, 143
  - centred, 32
communicator's
  - communication, 135
  - Language performance, 135
  - mental image, 25
community's Language, 59
competence
  - Grammar, 123-127, 129
  - performance dichotomy, 122
Complementarity
  - Principle, 145
  - Theory, 145
complementary aspects, 145
composite
  - features presentation approach, 114
  - of units of symbolisation, 13
concept
  - definition of, 44-47
  - fundamental unit of, 11-12
  - meaning of, 45-46
concepts, 45-50, 56
  - as semantic components of lexical units, 56
  - basic or fundamental units of thought, 56
  - specification, 49
conceptual
  - inconstancy, 50-54
  - indeterminacy, 47-49
  - Intentional, 9
  - semantics, 45
  - specification, 48
  - Theory, 45, 48
  - units, 59
conjunction, 109
Constituency of
  - Structural Symbolics, 106-107

- Symbolics, 100, 106
construct, 30, 33
context
  - dependent, 141
  - free approach, 143
  - free grammars, 122-123, 137
  - importance of, in Grammar, 129-136
  - independent Language, 143
  - sensitive, 3, 14
  - nature of Language, 123
  - phenomenon, 123
contextual
  - events, 144
  - factors, 35
  - knowledge of, 35
  - facts, 3, 134-135
  - Linguistic competence, 37
  - Semantics, 42
contingent factors, 35
contrastive
  - conceptual semantics, 50, 56
  - Propositional Semantics, 56-58
  - semantic studies, 57
conventional
  - media, 66
  - mental representation, 59
  - mode of segmentation, 61
  - name, 45-47
  - pictures, 66
core constituents, 34
Côte des Neiges, 142
COULMAS, F, 89
Cours de Linguistique Générale, 12, 118
Course in General Linguistics, 12
cultural
  - accident, 105
  - tool, 123

Danes, 53
Danish, 53
declarative
- sentence, 131-132
decodings, 134-135
deduction, 20
degrees of proficiency, 23
Delta State, 52
Derivational Theory of Complexity (DTC), 120-121
desert, 113
deterministic, 144
- theory, 142
diachronic, 2
Diachronics, 1
dialect, 52
digits, 103-104
direct means of communication, 20
domain of
- Semantics, 44
- Syntax, 85

EINSTEIN, Albert, 145
Elements of Graphetics, 101-102
emes, 99
emic level, 106
Emics, 99-100
Emiology, 106-107
empirical context, 144
English
- alphabet, 103
- free text, 57
- free translation, 71
- language communicatee, 57
- language community, 31, 45, 48-49, 53
- lexical and free translations, 57
- literal translations, 74, 76
- sentences, 77, 79, 130
- TL literal level of translation, 70

- TL semantic structure, 76
- TL thought, 71
- translations, 68
Equality of all Language forms, 104-106
essential constituents of nature of Language, 44
Etics, 99-100
exceptions, 29
experience, 24-26
experienced, 24, 26, 59
- reality, 25
experiences, 11, 22, 28
experimental graphetics, 102
expression mode, 105
extralinguistic
- communication skills, 24, 33-36
- skills of language context, 36
- competence, 37

Fabricatory Graphetics, 102
faculty, 118-119, 142
fictitious component, 11
fields of human preoccupation, 116
flight
- purpose of aircraft, 17
focus of investigation, 2
foreigner talk, 138
forms, 30
Free Translation, 52
freedom of choice, 143
French, 31
FRIES, C.C., 110
functional priority, 94-95
functional superiority of speech, 95

general means of communication, 21
general extralinguistic communication skills, 34
generative (constructional), 82

generative
- Grammar, 15-16, 37, 109, 121, 141
- (Grammar = Linguistics), 15-16
- Grammar School of Linguistics, 7
- Linguistics, 130
- scientific paradigm, 8
- (Syntax = Grammar), 81-84
- theory of Language, 8-11
- traditional grammar foundation of, 108
- or syntactic component, 10
- Semantics, 9-10

Generativism, 3, 5, 84
Generativist linguistic, 18
- Theory, 18-19
- failure of, 18-19

genetic
- graphetics, 102
- investigation, 101-102
- or Fabricatory Graphetic, 102

genetically programmed, 96
gennemic
- graphetics, 102
- investigation in Phonetics, 101

gestural
- language, 6, 99, 105
- language variety, 93

gestures, 99
gigantic vision, 118
global thought pattern, 66
GOATLY, A. 128
Grammar, 24, 37, 137, 143
- and Linguistics, 15-38
- and Pragmatics, 118-137
- as bipartite framework, 9
- goal of, 15
- models, 9
- as tripartite object, 9
- set of rules of, 10
- Structural Semantics + Structural Symbolics, 39-41
- study of Language structure), 8-9, 39, 41-42, 87
- (Textual Semantics + Textual Symbolics), 42, 87

Grammar and Linguistics, 8-38
Grammarian, 108
grammatical
- descriptions, 129
- Theory, 15
- tools or methods, 119

graph, 102
grapheme, 102
Graphemics, 100, 102
Graphesemics, 100
Graphetics, 100
- elements of, 101-102
- essential units of, 102
- principles of, 101

graphic
- language symbolisation types, 98
- particles, 103
- phrase syntax, 107
- sentence syntax, 107
- text syntax, 107

graphicles, 103
- analysis, 103-104

Graphics, 99-100
Graphology, 107
Graphomorphology, 107
Greek linguistic studies, 130
guesses, 134-135
gustatory (taste) symbolisation, 98

habitual, 59
- characteristic strategies, 30

HALLIDAY, M. A. K. 24
handicapped, 98

HEFFNER, R.M.S., 101
HEISENBERG, 145
HEISENBERG's Indeterminacy Theory, 145
Historical Linguistics, 1
historical priority, 92-93
HOOD, Robin, 76-77
human
- communities, 93
- languages, 90, 105
- mind, 118-119, 126
- societies, 93

idea (mental image), 45
ideographies, 93
Igbo, 31, 51-54, 60, 111
- language, 60, 66, 70
 - community, 54, 67
- grammarians of, 67
- people, 67, 70
- sentence, 68, 71, 74, 79
- SL community's world picture, 70, 73, 79
- thought pattern, 64
illocution
- level categorisation of sentences, 135
- types, 135
illocutionary
- categorisation, 129, 135
- classification, 132
- force, 135-136
 - specification, 136
- intentions, 135
- theory, 143
illocutive
- category, 133-134
- intent, 133-135
illocutively
- double-barrelled expression, 133
immediate
- context, 35

- of Language communication, 36
imperative, 130
- sentence, 130
Indeterminacy Theory, 145
Indian
- linguistic scholarship, 29
- linguistic studies, 130
indicated, 20
indicational, 20
- communication, 20
- communicative tools, 22
- means of communication, 23, 28
indicator, 23-24
indigenous Nigerian Languages, 53
information
- component, 139-140
- dichotomy, 139
- receiver-party, 17
- sender-party, 17
- type, 140
Instrumental
- Graphetics, 102
- Phonetics, 102
intellectual paradigms, 83, 108
intelligent performance, 3
intercommunication, 31
interpretive, 83
- Semantics, 10
interrogative sentences, 130, 132-133
intralinguistic
- communication skills, 23-24, 31, 33-34
 - definition of, 24
- competence, 37
- skills, 28
intrisically representational, 23
irrelevant, 29, 45, 66

Knowable by convention, 21
knowledge

- of language, 23, 33
- of world realities, 34

LAKOFF, R.T., 128
Language
- acquisition, 23
- act, 135-136
- Acts, 128
  - Theory, 128
- bicomponential phenomenon, 12, 14
- characterisation of, 6, 16, 39, 118-119, 140
- choices, 35
- communication acts, 3, 35
  - context, 36
  - nature of, 32
  - skills, 23
    constituents of, 24
    - extralinguistic communication skills, 24
    - intralinguistic communication skills, 23
    - peripheral constituents of, 34
- tool, 16, 23, 33
- communicative character of, 17
- communicator, 6, 24, 135
- communities, 41
- community, 26, 31, 34-35, 57-58, 60, 62-63, 66
- community's members, 30
- community's world picture, 74
- competence, 23, 121
- components of, 8-9, 11, 29, 98
- comprehension, 27-28
  - three Rs of, 27
- construction, 28
  - and comprehension, 25
  - three Rs of, 26
- content, 5, 40, 86
  - nature of, 28
  - symbolisation component, 4
  - thought component, 4
- context, 34, 127-129
- contextual part, 3
- contexture
  - knowledge of, 37
- core constituents of, 24
- data, 118
- definition of, 8, 11, 13
- distinguishable form
  - non-linguistic means of communication, 22
- dynamic nature of, 143
- elements, 96, 143
- equating speech to, 104
- faculty, 118-119, 126, 142
- form, 5, 29
  - units, 106
- forms, 66, 98
  - equality of, 104-106
- function of, 16

- generation, 9-10
    - study of, 39
- indicational means of communication, 19, 23
- indicational phenomenon, 22
- information receiver party, 17
- information sender party, 17
- intellectually vacuous, 17
- intrinsic nature of, 1
- is not speech, 90
- knowledge of, 23
- make up, 5
- meaning, 5, 9-10, 29
    - study of, 39
- means of communication, 27
- medium of, 96-97
- model of, 10
- nature of, 2, 3, 6, 18-19, 37, 90, 115, 128, 131, 138, 142
    - non-structural constituents, 6
    - structural constituents, 6
- non-structural essentials of, 4
- non-structural features of, 16
- object, 34
- performance, 23, 35, 53, 116, 128
- phenomenon, 3-7, 11
- representational means of communication, 19, 27
- representational semantic-symbolic potentiality, 13
- scholar, 50-51, 68
- scholars, 29, 120
- scientific study of, 14
- semantic or thought component, 13
- sides of, 12
- social phenomenon, 2
- sound, 9-10
    - study of, 39
- sounds
    - nature of, 41
- spoken variety of, 91
- standard characterisation of, 11
- structural description of, 137
- structural study of, 89
- structure, 3-4, 7-10, 16, 18, 36, 63, 119, 122, 128-129, 137
    - aspects of, 124
    - characterisation of, 9, 123
    - context free, 141
    - competence, 16
    - features, 37
    - knowledge of, 125
    - Linguistics, 37-38
    - study of, 137
    - theory of, 138
- study of, 84
    - symbolisation (symbolics), 14
- symbolic or symbolisation component, 13-14
- symbolisation, 64, 66, 89, 97
    - component of, 97
    - constituents of, 106
    - level of, 49
    - or form, 14
    - study of, 89
    - types, 98
- teachers, 33
- text, 34, 127-129
    - study of, 137
- textual part, 3
- texture, 3, 23-24, 34, 37, 146
- theory of, 8-11, 15, 32
- thought, 64, 66

- or meaning component of, 14, 41
- symbolisation of, 99
- thoughts, 30
- unit, 116
- units, 71, 127
- use of, 7, 23, 125
  - as a social tool, 7

Language Use, 16, 125, 137
- contextual facts of, 53
- knowledge of, 37
- study of, 127-128

Language users, 1-4, 32, 120-121, 123, 142

Language using
- communicating individuals, 23
- individuals, 4

Latin-derived, 103

Le Hasard et la Nécessité, 141

lexical-base of Grammar, 108-109

lexical
- categorisation, 110, 114
- category, 109, 112-114
- constituents, 139
- elements, 108, 110-111
- form, 113
- item, 71, 108, 110-116
- translation of sentence, 70
- unit, 122

lexicon and grammar, 108-117

LINDEN, 90

Linguistic
- abilities, 23
- analysis, 130
- communication, 23, 98, 134-135
  - distinctive character of, 19-23
- product, 142
- competence, 15-16, 33, 36-37, 53
- construction and comprehension, 24-27
- decodings, 134
- dependency, 64
- description, 2-3
  - framework, 130
- determinism, 63
- evolution, 1
- form, 115
- intuition, 48
- investigation, 84
- meaning, 115
- parameters, 139
- phenomenon, 1
- relativism, 64
- relativity hypothesis, 63, 66
- science, 101
- structure competence, 15
- studies, 91, 122, 140
- Theory, 6, 8, 15, 84, 127, 142
  - of Performative Linguistics, 11

Linguistics, 36
- as a science, 37
  - discipline, 2, 6
- as a social science, 6-7
- conduct of, 1
- development of, 127
- goal of, 2, 15
- scientific study of Language, 40, 43, 88
- (Semantics + Symbolics), 14, 86
- shape of, 2
- study of Language structure, 16
- study of thought (Semantics), 14

- sub-discipline of, 128
- (Textual Semantics and Contextual Semantics) + Textual Symbolics and Contextual Symbolics), 43, 88

Linguistics, 1, 49, 90. 127-128, 134, 143
literal translation, 57-58, 74-75, 80
Logical Form (LF), 9
LYONS, J. 91-92, 94, 96

mainstream didactic pronouncements, 82
material artifacts, 34
Meaning and the Structure of Language, 139
meaning
- component, 11
- or Semantic rules, 83

mechanics, 145
medium of Language, 90
memory lapse, 124
mental
- artifacts, 34
- construction, 41
- constructs – thought (or meaning), 38
- image, 25, 45
- pictures, 30
- reconstruction, 59
- representation of reality, 58

Microlinguistics, 127
minimal writing strokes, 102-103
Minimalist Programme (MP), 5, 9
misleading, 144
misnomer, 144
mnemonic value, 144
mode of segmentation, 59
model of Language structure, 127
modern Linguistics, 111, 114-117, 119, 127

- cardinal principle, 96
modern science
- theories of, 144
MONOD, Jacques, 141
Montréal, 141-142
morphological
- criterion, 111
- definition, 111
- means definition type, 111-112
- principle mode, 113, 115

Morphology, 49, 106-107
- study of word structure, 106

native user of a language, 47
natural Language, 57
Neogrammarian School of Linguists, 1, 6
neutral, 29-30
new information, 139, 141-143
NEWTON, Isaac, 144
Newtonian determinism, 144
Nigeria, 111
Nigerian languages, 51, 53
non
- human animal means of communication, 104
- Igbo people, 60

non-linguistic
- means of communication, 19, 22, 27
- status, 104

non-Linguists, 143
non-meaning
- changing transformations, 120

non-speech communication media, 90
non-structural
- studies, 41
- terms, 41

noun, 109-115
- phrase, 139

Nuclear

- cherics, 100
- Graphics, 100, 102-104
- Phonics, 100
- Semantics, 44, 47, 54-55
- Symbolics, 99-100

NWACHUKWU, 70, 79

OBASANJO, Olusegun, 28-30
obligatory, 37
OGDEN, 27
old information, 139, 141-143
olfactory (smell) symbolisation, 98
onomatopoeia, 29

paradigm, 11, 27
Particle
- cherics, 107
- Graphics, 107
- Phonics, 107
- symbolics, 106-107

parts of speech, 109-110, 113, 115
passive competence, 32-33
passive Language competence, 31-33
patently false, 93
PEARSON, B.L., 90
perceptual model, 122
Performative-competence dichotomy, 122
Performative
- Grammar, 118, 122-127, 129, 138
- Linguistics, 3-5, 21, 128, 143
  - characterising language, 11-14
  - Theory, 30

Performativism, 3
performer of the acts, 19
peripheral constituents of language communication skills, 34
PF, 9
phenomenon, 1

Philosophy, 145-146
phone, 102
phoneme, 102
Phonemes, 94
Phonemics, 100, 102
Phonesemics, 100
phonetic
- features, 110
- Form (PF), 9
- scripts, 94, 97
- value, 92

Phoneticians, 101
Phonetics, 49, 91, 100, 102
- definition of, 101
- divisions of, 102
- essential unit of, 102
- science of speech sounds, 101

phonic, 89
- phrase syntax, 107
- sentence syntax, 107
- Text syntax, 107

Phonics, 99-100
phonological (i.e. phonic), 89, 114
- component, 9
- constituent, 9
- or sound set, 82
- rules, 9-10
- surface component, 10
- unit, 111

Phonology, 9, 49, 107
- study of Language sound, 9, 39

phonomorphology, 107
phrasal Language unit level, 99
phrase
- cherics, 100
- forms, 54
- Graphics, 100
- meaningful form unit, 54
- phonics, 100
- structure, 116

- Symbolics, 99-100, 106
- Syntax, 106-107
- Thought Semantics, 54-55

Physiological Phonetics, 101
pictographies, 93
picturable, 116
Pidgin language, 138
PIKE, 101
poetic language, 18
post-semic levels, 106
potentiality, 13
PP, 120-121
Pragmalinguistics, 127
- Theory, 128

Pragmatic Problem (PP), 120-121
Pragmatics, 37, 49, 127-128
- contextual factors of, 129
- Contextual Semantics + Contextual Symbolics, 42
- criterion, 137
- study of Language use
- Theory, 128
- Use (or Contextual Semantics + Use (or Contextual) Symbolics, 42

Pragmaticist, 3
- perceptive, 3

Pragmaticist Movement, 128
preposition, 109, 113-115
presentation approach
- composite features, 114-115

primacy of speech, 91, 96
- principle, 5, 89

problematic, 110
procedures, 82
professional translators, 33
proficiency
- degrees of, 23

pronoun, 109
proposition
- definition of, 56
- meaning of, 56

- semantic constituents of phrasal units, 56

propositional
- level, 59
- semantics, 44, 54-56
- Theory, 56

psychoanalytic inferences, 63
psychological
- context, 35
- reality, 119, 126

psychologically real Grammar, 126

quantum mechanics of, 145
quarks, 144
QUERIDO, 141

R1, 25-28, 65
R2, 25-28, 65
R3, 25-28, 65
RAMBO, 46
real world of acts, 19-21, 23
realist, 4
realities, 30
Reality, 26-27, 41, 64
recalls (represents), 21
reconstruction
- of experienced reality, 59

reference, 25, 27, 65
reference by recalling, 26
references, 30
referend, 25, 27, 65
referends, 30
- meaning, 26

referent, 25, 27, 65
referents, 30
rejected, 91
Relativity Theory, 145
remote context for Language communication, 34
represent, 28, 30
representational, 21-23, 45

- and communicative code, 21
- communicative code, 22
- communicative tool, 22
- means of communication, 27
- nature of language, 64, 66
- relationships
  - distinctive character, 27-31
- system-structure, 11
represented, 5, 21, 28, 30, 46, 48-49
representer, 5, 21, 28, 30, 47
representing forms, 99
resemblance, 28, 30
RICHARDS, I.A., 27
ROBINS, R.H., 92
rules, 82
RUMBAUGH, D.M., 90

SAPIR-WHORF Hypothesis, 60-67
SAUSSURE, Ferdinand de, 1-2, 6-7, 12, 29, 110, 115, 118, 140
school of linguists, 8
science, 145-146
 - of speech sounds, 101
scientific
 - linguists, 6
 - paradigm, 1-2, 84, 119
 - theory, 124
SEARLE, J. R. 128
segmentation
 - mode of, 59
semantic, 114
 - base component, 10
 - component, 9, 121
 - constituent, 9
 - fact, 116
 - interferences, 53
 - intuition, 49
 - level, 26-27, 65, 116
 - or meaning set, 82

- or thought component, 12
- particles, 44, 47
- problem (SP), 120
- rules, 9-10
- symbolic, 12
- unit, 115
Semanticists, 49
Semantics and Grammar, 39-80
Semantics
- conceptual, 44
- domain of 9, 44, 48, 51, 81, 99, 104
- linguistics, 14
- Nuclear, 44
- Propositional, 44
- study of language meaning, 9, 39-40
- sub-discipline of, 50, 55-56
seme, 12
semes (in Performative Linguistics), 99
semic-level of Symbolics, 106
semic or meaning scripts, 95
Semics, 99-100
sentence
 - categorisation, 143
 - Cherics, 100
 - constructs, 115-116, 128, 132, 135-136
 - Graphics, 100
 - pattern, 135
 - Phonics, 100
 - structure, 136
  - typification, 136
 - structures, 139-140
 - Symbolics, 99-100, 106
 - Syntax, 106-107
 - Thought Semantics, 54-55
sentences
 - classification of, 130, 143
 - construction, 111
 - meanings of, 54
sentential language unit level, 99

sign
- components of, 11
- fundamental unit of language, 12
- language, 93
- sound form, 11
signs, 99
simplified language, 138-139
SL community's world picture, 68-80
social context for Language communication, 34
social tool, 134
sound
- component, 11
- medium of language, 90
- nature of, 97
- or phonological rules, 83
- recognition organs 97
- units of, 11
source language (S.L.), 50-51, 53
- community's world picture, 68-80
spatio-temporal arrangement in communication, 110
speech, 92-93
- acts, 128
- and symbolics, 89
- and writing, 91-97
   - study of, 89
- medium, 105
- organs, 96
- parts of, 109-110
- primacy of, 96-97
- sounds, 90, 96
  - science of, 101
- structure, 94
- study of, 91
spoken language, 5-6, 18, 91, 93, 96, 128
- sounds of, 41
spoken

- phonemes, 99
- variety of language, 91
STALLYBRASS, O., 35
state of affairs, 31, 66-67
Stoics of Greek antiquity, 92
structural
- Cherics, 107
- graphics, 107
- Linguistics, 2, 38, 130
- phonics, 107
- priority, 93
- strategies, 142-143
- symbolics, 88-89, 106-107
structure of
- Language, 17
- symbolisation, 25
- thought, 40-41
- writing, 93
study of
- Language symbolisation, 91
- speech, 89, 91
- symbolisation, 40
- thought, 40
Sub-disciplines of Semantics, 50, 55-56
subjectless, 58
subject-predicate, 139
suprasentential Language units level, 99
SWEET, H. 101
Swiss linguistic genius, 129
syllabaries, 95
symbolic, 98
- level, 26-27, 65, 116
- linguistics, 101
- representer, 47
Symbolics, 100
- and Grammar, 85
- character and constituency of, 106
- constituency of, 85, 100
- in Linguistics, 14

- science of Language form, 99
- science of language symbolisation, 98
- phrase, 99
- text. 99

symbolisation, 25-26, 29, 40-41
- character of, 97-101
- fundamental unit of, 12
- phonic aspect of, 104
- sound aspect of, 104
- structures, 24
- systems, 5-6, 97
- tactile type of, 98
- types, 98, 105
- units of, 13

syntactic, 114
- component, 9-10
- constituent, 9
- constructs, 9
- criterion, 114
- features, 115
- means definition type, 112
- or syntax set, 82
- structures, 9, 118-119
- unit, 115

syntacticist, 2, 15, 84
- approach, 84
- perspective of Language, 84

Syntax, 2, 5, 10, 49
- domain of, 85
- layers of, 106
- part of Symbolics in Linguistics, 85
- study of
    - external structuring of words, 85
    - Language generation, 39
- theory of, 8
- three layers of, 106

system of procedures, 82
system of rules, 82-84
system-structure, 13
- of symbolisation, 13

tactile (touch) symbolisation, 98
TAFI Alphabet, 103
target language (TL), 33, 50-51, 53, 68, 80
Teach Your Child to Write, 103
telegram language, 138
TERRACE, H.S., 90
text
- Cherics, 100
- Graphics, 100
- Linguistics, 3
- Phonics, 100
- Symbolics, 99-100
    - levels, 106
- syntax, 106-107
- Thought Semantics, 35-36

textual
- linguistics, 37-38
    - competence, 37
- Semantics, 42, 87
- Symbolics, 42, 87

theories of modern science, 144
theory, 128, 143
- of Language, 32
thought, 25-26
- and symbolisation, 24
- complexes, 57
- (or meaning), 40, 86
- patterns, 58, 63-64
- structures, 24

Three Rs
- of Language Comprehension, 27, 65
- of Language construction, 27, 65

TIME-LIFE, 90
Traditional

- Grammar, 91, 108-109, 111
- lexical categorisation scheme, 109
- theoretic errors, 109
transformational rules, 116
transformational
- component, 10
- Generative Grammar, 108
- Grammar, 120-121
- rules, 10
translatable, 51, 72
translation, 52
- convention, 71
translations, 57, 68
triangular model of concepts, 27
tripartite
- entity, 115
- object, 9
- scheme, 9

UL (Unknown Language), 57-58
- community, 58-59
Unified Linguistic Theory, 138
Universal laws, 144
Université de Montréal, 3, 138, 141
University of Benin, 5
Use
- linguistics, 38
- (or Contextual Conceptual Semantics, 44
- (or Contextual) Nuclear Semantics, 44
- (or Contextual) Propositional Semantics, 44
UWAJEH, M.K.C. 103, 105, 128, 133

variables, 35
verb, 109-110, 114-115
- phrase, 139
virtue, 45
visual
- Graphetics, 102
- (sight) symbolisation, 98
visualised, 24
visually handicapped, 98
vowel harmony, 51
- rules of, 51

warning, 136
Western civilisation, 140
WHORF, B.L., 60-61
word, 111-113, 116
world picture, 58, 60
- of language communities, 64, 66
- realities, 37
writing
- characters, 103
- copy of speech, 94
- invention of, 95
- marks, 96
- organs, 96, 102
- structure of, 93-94
- system, 103
  systems, 103
- units, 102
written language, 6, 91, 96
- shape, 92

Yoruba, 111

zoo language, 138

www.ingramcontent.com/pod-product-compliance
Lightning Source LLC
Chambersburg PA
CBHW051525230426
43668CB00012B/1744